# Life Lessons...

## My Journey in Faith

As seen through a gardener's eyes and everyday life experiences...

# LINDA KROPP

# Life Lessons...
## My Journey in Faith

As seen through a gardener's eyes and everyday life experiences...

Unless otherwise noted, all scripture is from the King James Version (KJV) of the Bible.

*God*

MANIFEST | PUBLISHING

www.GodManifestPublishing.com

This book and all other God Manifest Publishing books are available on Amazon.com.

Cover designed by Jonnathan Zin Truong
Interior designed by Jonnathan Zin Truong

For more information on foreign distributors, email
publishers@godmanifestpublishing.com
Reach us at on the internet: www.godmanifestpublishing.com

ISBN: 979-8-9920028-5-0
eBook: ISBN: 979-8-9920028-6-7

Printed in the United States of America.

# DEDICATION

Where to start?

I have read many dedications in books before, but now that the time is here for mine, it is different.

A lot goes into writing a book.

A lot.

It takes a lot of folks to come alongside you to make it happen.

My very first encouragers were my husband, Mitch, and our daughter, Elisabeth.

If they had not persisted, I would not have gotten this far. It has been a long time since my first writing in 1999 to the most recent in 2024.

I would also like to acknowledge the most influential person in my life, my mom, Shirley.

It is because of her that I came to faith in Jesus. I saw it lived out in her life on a daily basis. She took me to Church where I heard about God's love and purpose for me and I gave my life to Christ.

And then she supported my decision to follow God's leading into ministry.

My mom loved flowers and our home was always filled with them. I think she instilled that love for flowers and gardening in me.

She was never able to read any of my writings, she passed away before I began journaling. But I know that her prayers and her example have helped make me the person I am.

*So, I am loving dedicating this book to them.*

# ACKNOWLEDGMENTS

Gratefulness is so important.

A huge part of gratefulness is acknowledgment.

We are wise people when we realize that we have not gotten to the place we are without others.

I want to thank those in my life who have encouraged me to move forward with this book.

- My many friends over the years who have been blessed by the things I write and encouraged me to keep writing.
- Anita, who has been and continues to be a wise mentor and counselor and has encouraged me to go forward with the publishing of this Journal.
- My late mother-in-law, Johnnie Ruth, who always enjoyed my writings.
- My Thursday evening Bible Buddies Group from Atlanta Christian Church.
- My Women of Wednesday mentoring group from Atlanta Christian Church.
- Each of these ladies have encouraged and prayed for me.
- My sweet cousin and sister in Christ, Marilyn, who been a champion for me.
- My prayer partner, Kathleen, who has been my prayer partner for more than thirty years. We served overseas together and have seen many profound answers to prayer.

And a very special thank you to Marsha, a dear friend and fellow missionary, for her hours of typing these pages for print, that were written over a period of twenty-five years.

Thank you, Marsha.

# FOREWORD

What a fresh wind of the Spirit blows upon Linda as she shares her igniting experiences.

She shares with her readers from the greatest love of seeing things develop from seed to blossoms. She artfully takes these experiences of sowing and reaping and brings spiritual life to them.

Her spiritual metaphors bring life to all the secrets of seeing her gardens grow from her love of gardening. Linda's rich spiritual life flows through all her loving, sharing metaphors.

This book reveals Linda's love of seeing through the eyes of the Spirit her greatest love, Jesus.

Dr. Anita Mason F.M.F.T., D.Min.

Author of *Launch Out Into the Deep*

# WHAT PEOPLE ARE
# SAYING ABOUT THIS BOOK

"I have known Linda Kropp for fifty years. God has uniquely gifted Linda with the ability to identify God's presence in His creation and to aptly interpret a biblical life lesson for each of us observing a weed, a rose, or a vine.

It is refreshing and life-giving."

**Kathleen F. Hill**
*Coordinator of Straight Ahead Ministries, Nevada and Arizona*
*Institutional Chaplain (retired) at Florence McClure Women's Correctional Center,*
*Casa Grande Transitional Facility, and Jean Conservation Camp, all in Nevada*

"I have known Linda and observed her life for fifty years and have always been amazed by her faith and ability to receive God's lessons through small daily routines in her life.

So many of us are looking for the big move of God in our lives, and we miss His everyday appearances.

May Linda's personal writings in the book help us all to notice the presence of God in the simple routines of our daily lives."

**Marsha Van Wyk**
*Administrative assistant at Belmont Church, Nashville, Tennessee*
*Former missionary*

"I love it! I love it! I love it!"

**Marilyn R.**

# TABLE OF CONTENTS

SECTION

# ONE

*Early Writings*

# 1

## A RECIPE FOR CHARACTER

**ഔ** *Fall 1999* **ഝ**

Today I made some homemade vegetable soup for my family. It was going to be a very special soup because every ingredient was special. The ground beef was from our own steer; I cut up fresh parsley and potatoes and onions, lots of each to make the soup healthy. I peeled two bulbs of garlic and left the cloves whole for more flavor. I crushed fresh rosemary, ground some pepper, and seasoned the soup. I simmered the soup for hours, anticipating the end result. Last of all, I added my own canned tomatoes, green beans, and lastly, the most precious, my own canned corn. I only had a couple of jars left, so I only added the precious corn to special dishes. Now for the moral to my story.

After I added the last ingredient, the corn, I realized that the whole jar of precious corn was bad. I felt sick. All my work, all the time and ingredients, all ruined because the last, most precious ingredient was spoiled rotten.

The corn looked good, and it didn't smell bad, but when it was added to the other ingredients, the spoilage became obvious. At some point in the canning or preparation of the corn, bacteria got into the jar. I didn't see it, but it grew and eventually was the cause of spoilage. It made me think about how sometimes something may seem too small or insignificant to affect our hearts or minds, but it does.

As I stood at my kitchen stove, I feel like the Lord showed me this parallel to my own life. I had invested my time and hard work into preparing a healthy and delicious meal for my family to enjoy. I was very discouraged at the apparent waste of time and energy. And I feel the Lord quickened to my heart to realize that He has invested His time and work into my life. All the ingredients of my life blend together to make a woman that reflects the beauty of the Lord, but I can add or allow things in my life that will spoil the work that God is doing. And it doesn't matter whether the spoilage comes at the end; it still spoils the soup. So I must take care and walk worthy of the calling of the Lord.

# 2

## LESSON OF THE STRAWBERRIES

*ဢ June 25, 2000 ଔ*

This morning when I was out walking our dog, I walked by our strawberry patch. I noticed that it was overgrown with weeds. I could see some bright red strawberries poking their heads through the high weeds, but the weeds overshadowed almost every plant. I couldn't take it, so I stopped and started weeding. As I began thinking about what I was seeing, I saw such an analogy to the Christian life.

Our Heavenly Father is our master gardener. He says in John 15 that if we bear fruit, we are pruned. I have felt pruned many times in my life. It means that our Heavenly Father is watchful of us. I had just weeded that strawberry patch a few weeks ago, but it was almost overgrown in no time. I had not been watchful. Our Heavenly Father is. As I began pulling the weeds, I noticed several things.

Weeds were growing in our strawberry patch because conditions were right. The summer temperatures were high, and we had a lot of rain. When conditions are right for spiritual growth, conditions are right for weeds also. If our lives are dead and dry, nothing will grow. But if we desire to draw closer to the Lord, to yield our hearts to Him and live in His presence, then conditions are also right for weeds. Well, if the fruit of the Holy Spirit is love, joy, peace, patience, and long suffering as we see in Galatians 5, then the opposite would be the weeds. If we do not love, if we are not patient, if there is no joy in our lives, if we have no peace, then we have weeds. I do not feel these are the trials that James speaks about as trials that test our faith (James 1). No, I feel this is the battle we encounter when we desire to walk close to Jesus, when we face our carnal flesh.

I also noticed that the big weeds usually had only one root, but it was a big, strong root that went deep. But once I identified the source of the root and got a good grip on it and gave a yank, it was gone and then I could see the bright red fruit that was hiding.

There are a lot of lessons here. First, if the soil had not been fertile, the weed could not have grown so big. So when someone desires to know the Lord, the ground becomes fertile and weeds begin to grow. When the weeds begin to mature (get big), then we need to find the source.

If we are angry, if there is bitterness or unforgiveness in our hearts, these attitudes will produce ugly fruit in our lives. Once we identify the source (the root), then we give a good yank to rid ourselves of the weeds. How do we do that? That happens when we come to the Lord and confess our sins. First John 1:9 says, "If we confess our sins, He is faithful and just to forgive us our sins, and to cleanse us from all unrighteousness." We must yield to Him and ask Jesus to remove unwanted fruit from our hearts.

There was something else I noticed. Sometimes when I had identified the weed and began pulling, the root of the weed was intertwined with the strawberry fruit. I think sometimes in our lives, we let fruit grow and we think it's good fruit, but in actuality, it is not. This is self-righteousness. I think if we look at that word we will see a lot. By just switching the word around, it becomes *righteous self*. Doesn't that look ugly? Maybe someone has hurt us or hurt someone we love. We feel justified in holding a grudge. We may even take pride in how long and how hard we have held onto that grudge. But Jesus said that if we do not forgive others, He would not forgive us. That is pretty serious, especially when we realize that what we do now affects our eternity.

It is not only ugly fruit that results; unforgiveness leads us down a road that goes nowhere. Most people avoid others whose lives are filled with unforgiveness and bitterness. They are usually very unpleasant people to be around. Our Heavenly Father is actually filling our lives with beauty when He helps us get rid of unforgiveness and bitterness.

When we have fertile ground and we are bearing fruit, there can still be weeds growing intertwined with the good fruit. In one of Jesus's parables, He said there was a landlord whose enemy (Satan) had sown tares (weeds) among the wheat (good fruit). His servants asked what they should do. The landlord told the servants to let both the good fruit and the weeds grow up together and, at the harvest, gather the weeds and destroy them (see Matthew 13:24-30). I feel this shows that our Heavenly Father, the master gardener, allows weeds to grow in our lives. As we grow in the grace and knowledge of our Lord Jesus Christ, the Holy Spirit will reveal these areas to us and we can allow God to remove them.

The final lesson I observed was this: After the strawberry patch was weeded, I stood and looked at the difference in the final product. I was so proud. I feel this is how our Heavenly Father must feel when we allow Him to prune our lives and destroy the weeds. We cannot do it ourselves; only He can do this work because He is the master gardener.

*Note: September 3, 2000

I have just come from church, and I was in the middle of making lunch before some friends were due to come over. I have had a really rough week, and an incident at church only added fuel to the fire. As I sat down and re-read this little lesson, I felt the Holy Spirit gently correct my heart. I saw the ugly weeds in my life. When I was writing this earlier, I wrote with "the other guy" in mind. It is much easier to read and appreciate when you feel that it is not for you.

So I am adding this little postscript to remind myself of how God is at work in my life.

# 3

## A LESSON FROM MY GARDEN

ഇൗ *June 13, 2001* ൟ

I went to visit a friend the other day who loves to garden. While we were talking, I told her that the weeds in my garden had grown overnight! She encouraged me not to let the weeds get out of hand. I took her advice and started weeding my garden.

A few days have passed since then, and I decided to take advantage of the cool evening and enjoy my garden. The garden and the weeds had been growing, so I began pulling weeds again. I saw so many lessons. I looked at a plant that I had wanted in my garden that was now taking over precious space that other flowers needed to grow. I thought that it is like that in our lives sometimes. We invite things into our lives thinking they are beautiful and will enhance our lives, but then they take over. I think this can apply to friendships that we cultivate, showing that we allow ourselves to watch every area of life needs to be submitted to the Holy Spirit. We must be careful what we allow to be planted in our lives.

Another thing that comes to mind is busyness. If we allow ourselves to become over committed, even if with a good thing, other areas of our lives can suffer. Sometimes it is hard to say no. But it can be necessary if we find ourselves overwhelmed.

As I was pulling out the weeds, I remembered that my friend had beautiful plants that she said the Lord gave her because she hadn't planted them; they grew on their own. I was a little bit envious. I thought, "Why doesn't the Lord give me beautiful plants that I haven't planted?" Then I pulled up a couple of big weeds, and there in my garden was the very plant that my friend had. I hadn't planted it either. Then the Lord spoke to my heart. He told me I had not been in my garden to look for His gifts. If I had looked, I would have seen that He desires to give me the same gifts that He has given my friend. When I spend time with my Heavenly Father, there are always rich rewards and hidden treasures.

There were some tall, prickly weeds challenging me too! The roots were so deep that I had to use my shovel to get them out. I remember when they were very small and just starting to grow. I thought I would get them later; they were not such a bother. When they were small, they were soft and fuzzy, but when they were full-grown, they were hard and prickly. I feel like sin is like that in our lives. We allow small, soft, fuzzy things to take root and grow in our lives, not realizing that these same sins become hard and prickly when full-grown. And then they need to be dug out with a shovel, which always leaves a scar.

The last thing I saw as I worked in my garden was that while I was trying to clean out my garden, there were some busy bees keeping me from my work. The bees love my garden too. They don't mind me until I start disturbing them. It is like that in life. When we begin letting God work in our hearts and pulling weeds, there will be those around us to discourage us or to say, "Don't bother with that little sin. It won't hurt; just let it be!" But that is not what we should do if we desire to walk close to Jesus. We need to let Him weed the garden of our hearts.

# 4

## A LESSON FROM THE STORMS

*ಐ August 23, 2001 ೞ*

The phone woke me up at 1:10 a.m. It was my husband, Mitch. Our car had broken down, and I would have to drive forty minutes to pick him up at work. It was all right, I thought. But he wasn't finished with his news. "Oh, by the way," he said, "we just got word: we went out on strike." That was very unsettling for sure.

Then I went out walking this morning. It was so beautiful. I made my usual rounds of the flowerbeds and looked across the fields. It struck me how green the grass was. We had a very dry summer, and just two weeks ago, the grass looked like it was dying out. Now it was a beautiful emerald green. Then I remembered the three big storms we'd had over the last week. The grass had been so far gone that the few sprinkles that had come didn't faze them. It had taken some pretty major storms to revive the grass and the fields. Three storms. And the beauty it brought was unbelievable.

I felt the Lord spoke to my heart. He loves me so much that He allows storms in my life to revive me. Sometimes my heart becomes so dry. I may not even realize it, especially when dry hearts surround me. But when the storms come and my heart turns to Him, then beauty and life return to my heart.

It was a great encouragement to me to remember that I can look with confidence at this storm we are facing. It is for my good.

# 5

## ABOUT LIGHT

ഇ *April 14, 2002* ര

I have a very pretty scented candle. Today as I lit the candle, I noticed the votive glass. The candle threw off such a pretty light because the glass was etched. I thought that was such a parallel of my life as a Christian.

The Bible says my life should be a sweet fragrance to the Lord. (2 Corinthians 2:15)

The candle has to be lit (on fire) before you can smell the fragrance. I also am a light in this dark world, but it requires fire.

As the glass threw off a beautiful light because of the etching, my life shines beautifully when I allow the Lord to etch my life. Just as the potter molds the clay, Jesus carves His character into our lives. Our trials are His etching. It was the etching in the glass that set it apart and made it so beautiful. It is allowing God to work His character in us through trials that will set our lives apart.

When I walked out of the room, I turned off the light switch. I looked back at the candle; it now shone brighter because of the darkness. The light was so calming in the daylight, but when I turned off the room light, then the candle really served its purpose. It gave off a beautiful light and fragrance in the room. That is how we are to be. Our duty is to be a light to the lost that live in darkness around us, and we need to shine brighter because of the darkness. Then others might see Jesus, the true Light of the World, in us (John 8:12).

# 6

## A CEDAR TREE

*ജ September 10, 2002 ര*

On my way back from the mailbox this morning, I stopped under the evergreen tree in our front yard. I love to take a pine branch and break a small twig off and smell the fragrance. I reached up and broke off a small twig from the tree to smell the cedar fragrance. It wasn't very fragrant, so I broke the twig again and crushed the needles between my fingers. There still wasn't any scent. I was frustrated and disappointed. Then I looked up … I wasn't standing under a cedar tree.

There are so many lessons here. First, I could not expect to get the fragrance of cedar from any other tree besides a cedar. This applies to how we look at people. Sometimes we expect people who do not know Christ, to have the character of Christians. Without someone being born again and the Holy Spirit living in their heart, at best they can only be nice people. We should not expect those who do not profess to know Jesus as their Lord and Savior to act any other way than lost. They can't.

Secondly, when I wanted more fragrance from the tree, I crushed the needles. My instinct told me that by crushing the needles, their scent would be released. That is how it is in our lives. Our Heavenly Father knows that only by crushing us will the sweet fragrance of the Holy Spirit be released.

All this insight, and I was only walking back from the mailbox! I love you, Lord!

# 7

## THE WALL

*⊷ July 12, 2003 ⊶*

Sometimes when I am in the garden or just going about my daily routine as a wife and mother, the Lord will speak to my heart. He will use everyday things that I am familiar with, just as Jesus did in His parables. He spoke to everyday people using whatever was part of their lives. That is the way Jesus speaks to me.

Today, the Lord was doing such a work of grace in my heart. There was a family known to us that recently lost their fourteen-year-old son in a motorcycle accident. From the moment I heard of the accident, I had such a burden for these dear people and their loss. A few days ago, a friend invited me to go with her to visit the family. I had been praying for an opportunity as the Lord would lead me to minister to them.

While we were there, I was able to share with them of God's comfort in my life when our first daughter, Amy, died a few hours after she was born. I shared about a moment a few months after Amy died when I was standing in our bathroom, not breathing. It was like having a baby and the pain was so great that you couldn't breathe, and someone would say, "Breathe now." I remember thinking that day, "If I can just keep breathing, make myself breathe, just until I make it through this, I will be okay." I had never experienced grief like that before.

I remember when I was growing up, I wanted to be two things when I grew up: a wife and a mother. I had wanted children, lots of them, ever since I remember remembering. I shared with these dear folks that sorrow. And the sorrow that came a year and a half later when our second daughter, Katie, died at birth.

It's been eighteen years since Amy died and almost seventeen since Katie died, but when I opened my heart to share the grief, it was so familiar, like it was yesterday. I wanted to share with these parents who had lost their son that God's tender love and mercy had brought me from such despair and hopelessness to a place of wanting to wake up in the morning and just go on.

When my husband told me that he felt the Lord was going to give us another child, I said it would have to be his faith; mine was …

not gone, but not enough to carry me through. After burying two daughters and having two miscarriages, I was scared to try again. He wasn't, and I love him for that.

I am pretty sure I know the exact moment I got pregnant with Elisabeth. I knew. I just knew. God graciously gave us our third daughter, Elisabeth. But … now I had to learn to live with a child. I knew how to live with losing a child: shut down. Now I had to overcome my fear of losing the only daughter we had been allowed to keep, the only one I ever heard cry. I needed help.

Sharing my grief and sorrow over the deaths of our two daughters forced me to touch the areas of my heart that had been closed off for a long time. I hadn't allowed visitors to this part of my heart; it was too hard, too painful. I had told of losing Amy and Katie, but I would not allow anyone to see the deep hurtful part. It was like I had been telling a story in the third person. The Lord forced my hand. He knew what would happen when I reached out to comfort others from the storehouse of goodness and comfort that He has filled my life with. I would find the wall…

There were things in my life that were very painful. It was humanly impossible for me to repair the damage. So I went before my loving Heavenly Father, the Great Physician, in prayer. I needed a specialist, a heart surgeon. I needed Jesus.

At about the same time, I noticed a new stain on our downstairs hall ceiling. We had noticed a few months ago that we had a leak. My husband talked to a couple of men who are knowledgeable about this type of leak, and they advised him. Nothing more happened, so we assumed it was taken care of. It wasn't. A few days ago, we had some very powerful storms come through our area. The storms dropped more than five inches of rain in just a few days.

There was a lot of water damage done around us. At first, we didn't notice the second stain on the ceiling. Today, I did. My first thought was that I had thought it had been fixed. But then in that split second when the Lord speaks to your heart and you finally understand something, I felt like the Lord said, "The damage was never fully repaired. The partial fixing would hold through the small showers, but when the big storms came, and they would, a partial fix wouldn't do. It needed a master carpenter."

I had been trying to fix something in my life that had been broken. I didn't break it. Someone else did. But I was the one that needed the fixing. I needed to forgive someone that had hurt me in such a way that I just couldn't repair the damage. I tried on my own for a while. That only left me frustrated. Then very slowly, without my even realizing it, I built a wall of protection around my heart. A wall, not a pretty rose trellis that gave off a sweet fragrance. My wall was gray, ugly, and scarred. It wasn't straight and tall and uniform. It was uneven and broken down in many places. There were weeds growing, blocking out the Son. Without the Son's warmth, nothing of beauty would grow and last. I had never let anyone see the wall. I didn't know it was there myself until today.

Where did all this come from? I have been a believer for many years. I love Jesus. I have tried to let Him work and refine my life as a silversmith refines the trinkets and rough silver to create beautiful jewelry. How did I let a wall of unforgiveness build around my heart? I love my family. I love my husband. I love our daughter. My wall had not kept me from loving others: I was a Christian, and it was in my new nature as a believer to love others.

My wall had kept me from letting others love me. It had blocked out the rays of the Son and kept self-worth and self-acceptance from growing in my life. And because I really did not see how valuable and precious to my Heavenly Father I was, I tried to find that love and acceptance in others. I didn't find it. It wasn't there. God never intended for anyone besides Himself to fill the void of our hearts, my heart, that belong only to Him. That is why no one ever did. They couldn't.

Wow! When I saw that ... the prison doors opened for me! A wall uglier than the Berlin Wall dissolved in an instant. I knew I had found peace, real heart peace, that had lain just beyond my deepest longing for so long.

My Jesus is life, and without Him, there is no life at all. You may walk around, breathe, function in your role in life, but without Jesus as the love of your life, you can never be complete. I love Him so much. I cannot tell you how much He means to me. And I can't take credit for that! The Bible tells me that I only love Him because He first loved me.

I know that whatever burden in life you carry, Jesus will help you.

Jesus said that His yoke is easy and His burden is light (Matthew 11:30). God, our Heavenly Father, knows us, He created us and He will not give us more than we can bear any more than we could do that to our own children. Although I had to face some very painful situations in my life, I knew that the Lord was not going to give me more than I could handle.

And that is a comfort.

It has taken me less than two hours to put this on paper. It could have taken less time, but I cried a lot. It was a story that was written in my life over a period of years. If you are a believer, if you know Jesus and His mercy and you are carrying deep hurt and sorrow, don't let it take years to go to the Lord with it. Go now. If someone has hurt you—maybe you have forgiven them, but your soul is scarred—come to the Lord. He will heal you.

If a robber breaks down the fence surrounding your home and you don't plant something beautiful in front of the broken fence, it will cause you sorrow each time you look at it. But if you plant a beautiful, fragrant rose bush in front of it, one day the place of your sorrow will become a place of great beauty and joy.

After Amy died, someone told me that when you break a bone, that broken place becomes the strongest part of that bone after it heals. I found great comfort in that thought. Only Jesus can heal our sorrows. Whether they be the death of someone we loved or the separation of family or friends through strife, Jesus gave us the answer.

He said, "I am the way, the truth, and the life" (John 14:6). He is the answer.

# 8

## LISTENING FOR THE WHIRLWIND

*ঙ August 17, 2003 ଔ*

"Then the Lord answered Job out of the whirlwind." Job 38:1

I like to get up before anyone else in the house stirs to have a cup of hot tea and my quiet time with the Lord. I usually sit at the kitchen table and look out at our backyard. We have a beautiful backyard. It backs up to a cornfield. Each season has its own beauty, so it never gets old to me. Our vegetable garden is next to the field, so it's easy to see its transformation throughout the spring planting, summer growth, and the fall harvest. The Lord has helped me understand the seasons of my life by watching the example He has given us in nature's order.

As I looked out the glass door that faces the field this morning, my view was blocked by a large old peach tree lying on its side in our backyard. It looked awful. A few of our neighbors had commented on why we hadn't cut it down. We had had a summer storm and lightning had struck and split it right down the middle, but it had not severed it from the root. Before that, we'd had some very powerful winds, and the tree had withstood these, but the last storm with the lightning was just too much for the old tree...

It was my husband's idea to keep the tree. At the time it was hit, the tree was loaded with fruit. It was early in the season, so the peaches were very small and very hard! I thought it was a total loss. Too bad too—the neighbors said the tree had more fruit this year than it had in several years. My husband wanted to give the tree a chance. He said we were only about eight weeks away from harvest, so we could wait and see if it makes it? Okay.

But as the weeks passed and the grass grew among the limbs that could not be reached with the mower, I tried to convince my husband to please get rid of the eyesore in our backyard. I told him, "Another neighbor asked me why we have a tree lying on its side in the middle of our backyard." Peer pressure did not faze him (it bothered me though).

You see, he saw something that the others could not; he saw the fruit that was slowly maturing among the branches. You could not see it from far away; you needed to get close and look among the leaves. It took effort. He knew that the tree was still connected to the root, and although it appeared to be down and dying, it wasn't. It was just slow growing. Whenever someone took the time to ask about the tree, we always explained and shared our (his) vision. But not too many people asked. They just drove by and wondered what on earth we were doing with the dead tree.

It has been almost two months since the storm took the tree down. It is now full of the most beautiful, plump peaches I have ever seen. (I think the fact they are our peaches makes me a bit prouder!) As I sat looking at that old tree and thinking of the delicious fruit we were now enjoying, I was struck by the thought that if it had not been for my husband's willingness to be patient and wait, well ...I remember how impatient I was after the storm. If someone, anyone would have taken my advice, there would not be any delicious fruit right now.

How true that is in life. It wasn't the first big storm that took that tree down. We had a season of storms, some not more than hard rains. It was the second big storm that took that old tree down. It is like that for some believers. They are able to weather the hard rains, strong winds, and maybe one big storm, but then a second storm hits. It's like a lightning bolt: it splits their lives down the middle and knocks them on their sides. It wasn't able to uproot them, make them leave their faith, but they are no longer standing. It may appear they are not worth investing our time and energy in anymore. They don't seem to be growing; they are just lying on their side.

How wrong we can be when we do not heed the prompting of the Holy Spirit. When we judge from our own reasoning and are not merciful and tenderhearted toward those who are hurting or seemingly lifeless in Christ, we are the ones who lose out. There is precious fruit here, so let's not overlook these opportunities.

I realized that it was not my fruit from that tree we were now enjoying; it was my husband's. It was his patience and vision, and we were enjoying it. I am so proud of him for standing alone and waiting for the harvest. How grateful I am that the Lord is patient with me and that through life, He teaches so much about how to live and love others.

My day doesn't stop here, I then headed outside to check on other things growing in our yard.

I decided to check on our pumpkin hill. We had a mound of dirt next to our garden, and we planted our pumpkins there. They have done great. It is very beautiful to see the vines cascading down the mound and sending runners out into the yard. They look like a star with bright orange blossoms that open up early in the morning. As I walked out to turn the water sprinkler on so that I could water before the sun got too hot, I realized that the sprinkler had been left on from yesterday evening's watering. My first thought was our water bill! But as I looked at the vines before me and all the pumpkins that had seemed to double in size overnight, the water bill didn't seem to bother me as much.

What a lesson for me. My plants needed water. I didn't realize it. The leaves were huge and a bright green. The vines were loaded with lots of pumpkins. I was watering according to my gardening books, but my efforts only allowed my plants to survive. God's watering caused them to grow.

Then back inside to check on the peach butter I was making. I was trying a modified recipe to make easy peach butter. I usually don't make fruit butter because it takes a lot of time, and I am busy when the fruit is ready to be worked up. I thought I would experiment this year with some peaches that someone had given me. When people know that you can your own produce, they often will pass on fruit or vegetables that are very ripe. They would rather give the produce away to someone who will use it rather to let it go to waste.

These peaches were almost over-ripe and needed to be made into jelly quickly. So I modified a simple apple butter recipe, using a slow cooker instead of the faster stovetop method. The previous night, I had cleaned the peaches and put them on to cook down. This morning, they had been cooking for fifteen hours.

I now needed to put the cooked peaches on the stove for the final cooking down. When I put the peaches on the stove, I turned the burner up very high to get them processing quickly. I turned to tidy up the mess this had made in the kitchen. I got distracted. Suddenly, I could smell the peaches beginning to scorch; I quickly went to the stove and adjusted the burner.

The Lord spoke to my heart in that moment when I thought I was going to lose the hours of work I had put into the peaches. I had been impatient. This job was taking a long time, and I was trying to speed it up. Because I was not willing to let the fruit cook at the correct temperature, I almost lost all my work, the time of cleaning and preparing and hours of cooking because I was impatient.

James tells us that we should let patience have her perfect work. (See James 1:4.) How important patience is: it can be applied to every area of daily life. The Lord had helped me; I didn't lose all my work and time and effort. And I look forward to blessing friends and family when we share the finished product. Thank you, Lord, for helping me.

I am sharing these thoughts and workings of the Holy Spirit in my life because others have shared with me that they don't feel God speaks to them.

I am reminded of Job 38:1.

Maybe they have not learned to listen in the whirlwind.

# 9

## PRUNING: A LIFE LESSON

*ᕲ July 16, 2004 ᕳ*

Sometimes starting what I want to write is the hardest. I have things I want to get on paper, but I don't know where to begin, so … I have to backtrack to the beginning.

We are having a beautiful summer. Spring was early and cool; a pleasant summer followed on its heels. I have been able to put the finishing touches on my Mother's Day pond. We started it on Mother's Day last year and finished it up this year with an eight-foot windmill. I have colorful miniature rose bushes planted around it and many of my other favorite flowers. It is so relaxing to go out in the cool morning and water the flowers and check out the pond. I usually take my garden scissors and clip off (prune) the dead flowers from my plants. Little did I realize how many life lessons I would see in my morning watering today.

There is a gardening expression called *dead heading*. It may be used in other ways, but in gardening, it means to pinch off the flower or leaf that has already bloomed and is dying. There are at least two reasons for doing this that I can think of: One is to help the plant grow better. The plant will continue to use its energy to send nourishment to the dead flower if it remains, leaving less to support new growth. Second is that it looks prettier. A plant may have a lot of flowers and blooms and from a distance look very nice, but when you get close and see lots of dead flowers mixed in, it spoils the appearance.

For these reasons, I use the time that I water to check out my flowers. I pinch off old or dead flowers and break off any dead stems. I used to just use my thumb and pinch and twist off, which is easy if the flower is a mum or a petunia. But one day, it was the rose bush that needed dead heading. Ouch! It wasn't easy. I got my fingers pricked a few times before I thought, "This hurts. I'll get my scissors. I will carry them with me, and when I see I need them, they will be handy." I needed the right tool for the right pruning job. But when it came to the thick stems that had to be cut away, my scissors weren't sufficient. I took my shears. They were heavy duty. This is such a great way to start the day!

Then usually I walk back into the house and life begins. My family gets up (usually hungry), I have a list of daily chores that need to be started, and so I forget my garden flowers. But one day, I was trying to get things done and my "little" brother—he's actually just younger—came by to pick up some things. I was busy, and he was interrupting what I was trying to do. I became so impatient with him. (I think there is a special impatience that only brothers can bring out! I'm not totally sure though.) After he left, I felt so bad. I wondered why it seemed like I always got so impatient with my brother.

Then the Lord spoke to my heart. God was using my brother to prune my life. He was a special tool. With my friends or neighbors, I would try not to show any impatience I might be feeling, but my brother seemed to get to the heart of the matter. That was the place God was concerned about: my heart. It is out of the abundance of my heart that my mouth speaks, and God, my Heavenly Father, saw there were places that needed His pruning. So, he used someone who loves me— my brother—to expose the hidden impatience that He wanted out of my life.

Wow! It was like turning on a bright light in a dark room. I looked at this interruption so differently. I can't honestly say I welcomed it, but I saw a purpose in it and it changed my whole attitude. After I saw God's hand in this, I made a conscious effort to be kinder and more patient with my brother.

A few days later, I was watering in the morning and noticed the hanging basket our daughter had given to me for Mother's Day this year. It is beautiful. It is very special because it is a very thoughtful gift from her. It blooms profusely, but only when it is watered every few days. It had been a few days since I brought my scissors and trimmed the old flowers off, so this morning, I thought I would do that. It had grown since I got it, and there was a lot of old stuff: leaves, blooms, stems.

As I thought about this, the Lord spoke to my heart with this thought. This basket needed a lot of pruning because there had been a lot of growth. Another wow! If God is pruning my life, it is because there is growth. I was so encouraged. Pruning is not a bad thing. It means we are growing, and the master gardener is helping us. The dead things in our lives draw precious energy that we need to support new growth (those areas where we are letting God work, yielding to Him). It is actually easier for us when we are not carrying around old stuff. Our lives can more easily reflect the beauty of life when our hearts are fully surrendered to Jesus. Others can see our fruit and not be distracted by old stuff.

# 10

## SUNDAY MORNING

*ജ July 18, 2004 ഇ*

I love to get up and take a walk around the flower garden before I get ready for church. This morning as I walked, I remembered a visit I had with a friend on Friday. I noticed the beautiful flowers lining the sidewalk to her front porch. The beds were filled with tall colorful petunias, lavender, and snapdragons.

The plants were volunteers, a term that means they came up on their own from seed dropped the year before or even the year before that. Sometimes birds will carry the most beautiful seeds and drop them in your garden or your yard. Or the seed dropped from something you planted yourself will sprout next year, or it might even lie dormant for a few years and then when there is a growing season where conditions are just right, you will find them popping up.

I just love it when that happens. I spend a lot of time planning, buying, and planting the flowers and vegetables that we grow, and when a beautiful flower or tomato plant returns on its own, I love it! It's like God planted it for me. As I was thinking about that, I remember noticing how these beautiful petunias were growing up alongside this plant that looked like lavender. The petunias were long and very fragile; the other plant was tall and sturdy.

I saw such an analogy to our lives. I felt like the Lord spoke to my heart that that is how He plants in our lives.

The apostle Paul says in Romans 15:1, "We then that are strong ought to bear the infirmities of the weak." And he makes another reference in 1 Thessalonians 5:14, "Support the weak, be patient toward all men." Wow! How different our world, our towns, our families, our marriages would be if we let those two little verses fill our hearts—my own heart.

In nature, God put these beautiful, fragile flowers intertwined with the strong, bold, sturdy support plants. Then when the rain beats down or a strong wind blows (and we have strong winds in Illinois), they would be supported. I could see in my own life the very same example.

There have been times in my life when I felt like I was standing on the beach in a hurricane and wave after wave seemed to hit and I couldn't get my breath. I would turn and my loving Heavenly Father would plant someone strong and sturdy to reach out and help return my heart to Him and find my way back to Jesus, the Light in the darkness, the Comforter in sorrow and the only source of true wisdom when we are confused.

I also realized that the Lord puts people in my life who are weak and need my support. Our responsibility is to turn them to Him. For in ourselves, we are not the answer.

Jesus is.

We can support only when we know we are not the answer.

Jesus is.

"God is ...a very present help in trouble" (Psalm 46:1).

I think many times we avoid people who are needy, but God may have put them in your life because you are to be a support for this time. We cannot do this in our own strength.

Again Psalm 46:1 begins, "God is our refuge and strength."

When I garden, I don't make the flowers and vegetables; I don't even make them grow. God does. I just plant them (sometimes).

If God is calling you to help someone, it's not your work; it's His. You can trust Him to give you the strength to do what He is calling you to do. Don't trust in your own feelings or wisdom; obey His Word that tells us to "trust in the Lord with all thine heart; and lean not unto thine own understanding. In all thy ways acknowledge him, and he shall direct thy paths" (Proverbs 3:5–6).

I think it is also important to realize that in our time of weakness or pain, when the Lord puts others in our path to encourage and strengthen us, it is for His glory. It is His loving kindness that is touching us, and we need to go to Him and thank Him. We must not look to others for the help and support we feel we need.

No one will be able to heal a broken heart or comfort the deepest sorrow except Jesus. He may use others to reach out to you, but it all comes from His loving hand.

# GREEN BEANS & NEW POTATOES

ᔖ *July 18, 2004* ଓ

Today as I was preparing lunch for my family, I was having such a sweet fellowship with the Lord. As I was praying for those on my heart, I could sense the Lord's encouragement and presence. I was making the first batch of the season of green beans and new potatoes. A neighbor had shared their bounty of green beans (I didn't put any out this year), so this was a real treat for us. Green beans and new potatoes are one of those summer harvest dishes that always remind me of my mom. It was a reward for all the hard work she had put into her garden. It has a special taste that you just can't get from any store. If you have ever eaten them, you know what I mean.

I put everything on the stove to cook and decided to go outside for a while. The kitchen was heating up from all the cooking. I walked out to the pool to water a big flowerpot we had out there. The hose doesn't reach it, so I need to make a special trip to keep it watered. I have several other flowers like that. This morning as I was making the rounds to water, the Lord spoke to my heart this thought: how important it is to be planted close to a water source.

Jesus is the living water. He said so in John 4:10–11 and John 7:38. I must stay close to the water source. Those things that are planted farthest from the source are seldom watered. It takes extra effort. If I am short on time (which happens), I won't put on the extra hose it takes to water the things that are out of reach.

I can stay close to the water source, Jesus, by keeping my heart in right fellowship through reading and meditating on God's Word (the Bible) and by allowing the Holy Spirit to search my heart in quiet, private prayer. I have found these things to be essential in walking with the Lord. God's Word truly is a light and acts as a lamp for our path (Psalm 119:105). When I read my Bible, the Holy Spirit uses it to reveal my heart. Sometimes I can fool myself into thinking it's all okay, but through allowing the Holy Spirit to work in my life, I see how things really are. I am so thankful to God that He has not left us to try and figure things out on our own. He will help and guide us if we turn to Him.

I ended up staying outside a little longer than I should have. I knew I had things cooking, and I thought, "Lord, please don't let anything burn." Well, I think praying like that is like asking God for rain but praying that it wouldn't be wet. It is pretty unrealistic. God will not go against His own laws of nature. Rain is wet. If you put fire under something long enough, it will burn. And it did; the new green beans and potatoes had already started to burn when I got in the house. I am thankful that I was able to save most of them. But it was an old lesson to me to be watchful and not wasteful.

I felt that at one point the Lord had reminded me to go check on the food, but I was distracted. I think that happens a lot in our lives. The Holy Spirit will remind us how to walk, and we must not get distracted but heed His prompting. I know that when we sit down to lunch today, I will have a little more than green beans and new potatoes on my plate.

# 12

NEW GLASSES

*ဆ July 20, 2004 Ꮳ*

Today when I started to open my Bible and read, I realized that my glasses needed cleaning. I turned fifty this year. I had my first traffic ticket and my first flat tire, I hit a deer for the first time, and I had my first ride in a tow truck. Actually, my life must have seemed uneventful to others before now.

Another first was getting glasses—with bifocals. I had squeezed by for several years with the non-prescription reading ones. Then onto prescription glasses, but after a year or so, I needed stronger ones. They are quite expensive, and someone told me to go to Wal-Mart and get the $1 kind. Well, it must have been a while since they were there because when I went to Wal-Mart, they were $10. Maybe they needed glasses to see the extra zero.

I did this for several years, but my eyes weren't the only things getting fuzzy; my memory was too. I always seemed to be misplacing stuff. I didn't lose things; I just misplaced them. One day, I was at Save-a-lot and noticed they had the same reading glasses I had bought for $10 for just $1. Wow, I could have lots of spares. I would keep them in strategic places: with my Bible, in my purse, by the phone. So, I bought spares, five of them. That was fine until this year. I went to slide my glasses up on top of my head and there was already a pair there!

My husband and daughter insisted that I get real glasses. I caved into their pressure, and I got my first pair of real glasses with bifocals, the kind you have to wear all the time. It was an adjustment. Once I began wearing my glasses all the time, I realized how out of focus everything had been. My glasses now brought things into focus.

Life is like that. Until we give our lives to Jesus, we think we are seeing clearly, but when the Holy Spirit dwells in our hearts, we begin to understand and see God's perspective (focus) on things. The Bible says God's thoughts are higher than our thoughts, and His ways are higher than our ways (see Isaiah 55:9).

Also with my new glasses, I could see clearly when I was looking directly at something. In Proverbs 4:27, God tells us not to look to the right or to the left, but to look straight ahead, to keep our focus on Him.

The last thing I realized was how I had taken the precious gift of sight for granted for so many years. All my life, I could turn my head, look up and down, and look quickly out of the corner of my eyes and see. Now I have to wait until my eyes are in focus with my glasses.

Psalm 139 says we are fearfully and wonderfully made. I now make it a point to thank my loving Heavenly Father for His precious gift of sight, and I am grateful for all the years that I had clear vision.

When I started to read this morning and had to clean my glasses, it was because they were soiled from yesterday. I get up to clean them every morning, the first thing. That is how it is with my spirit. Yesterday can spoil our spirits, and we need to clean our spiritual eyes (our hearts) before we start a new day. Reading God's Word, the Bible, and praying can cleanse our hearts and help us to see clearly. Because God's Word is alive, quick, and powerful (Hebrews 4:12), it will accomplish its purpose. The Holy Spirit will help us keep a pure heart before the Lord. So, as I clean my glasses each day to see this world more clearly, I bend my knee and ask God to search my heart (Psalm 51:10) so that I may see Him more clearly.

# 13

## A WORD ABOUT WEEDS
## ... AND BEING VIGILANT

*ᔆᔆ July 28, 2006 ᔆᔆ*

We had a huge rain last night. This was about the third one in as many days. Everything is greening up nicely. We had been out of town for a few days, and when we had left, we were in desperate need of rain for the crops, the gardens, and the grass.

We finally got the rain we needed, and I went to check on things growing in our yard. I could see the bright red blackberries ripening from the kitchen window. I was so eager to get outside and make my rounds. But I was not prepared for what I saw. From a distance, everything looked okay, but as I got closer, I could not believe what I was seeing. Japanese beetles covered the leaves of my beautiful and fragrant climbing rose bush, my blackberries, the raspberries, and the grapes. They were even crossing over to my large grasses.

I came inside and got down on my knees and asked the Lord to show me what I should do to get rid of them. An idea came to mind, so I started outside with a zip-top bag, scissors, and a large leaf bag. I would put the zip-top bag over the leaf that was loaded with beetles and cut it off so that it would drop undisturbed in the bag. It turned out to be too much for the rose bush. I finally cut almost all the leaves off to stop the beetles from destroying it. If anyone was watching— and someone usually is in our small town (I say that lovingly: we all watch out for each other)—I'm sure they did not understand what I was doing. It probably did not look like I was trying to save my rose bush. But I knew why I was doing it.

I think it must be like that with our Heavenly Father. Our lives may be being devoured by something, but we are unaware of it. Trials (pain) that are meant to trim back our lives occur, and we stand back and wonder what the master gardener (our Heavenly Father) is doing.

I had to use some very big pruning shears to cut the rose bush back. I didn't have any, so I went to my neighbor to borrow some; my scissors were not sturdy enough to do the job. I can think of some times in my life when I felt like the Lord used some pretty big shears on me. I had to go to the main stem on the rose bush to stop the damage from the beetles. I think God must use the big shears (trials, tests) when He is cutting back deeply to prevent greater damage to our lives.

On my way back inside, I stopped to pick a few weeds. I have discovered that if I pull a few weeds every day, they do not get out of hand as quickly. Sometimes that still happens, but not as often. It is like that in our lives also. If we keep our hearts close to Jesus and let Him pull those weeds daily through prayer, reading the Bible, and fellowshipping with other believers, it is less likely that our lives will get out of control.

I noticed that the weeds that were under several inches of mulch were the easiest to pull. Their roots had to grow through a thick layer of mulch, and they were long and fragile. I like those; one yank and they are gone. I think that is what prayer does in our lives. It covers us. If unwanted things do grow, they have to grow through prayer. If we are praying and confessing our sin before the Lord, not much unrighteousness can grow. As a good gardener will continually add layer after layer of mulch to keep the weeds out, a wise believer will continually add layer after layer of prayer and confession of known sin in his or her life to keep the weeds (sin) out.

Just as the abundant rain was good for my garden, it provided the same excellent growing conditions for weeds. If there was a contest (a cash prize would be nice) for the biggest weeds, I would make it to the final four—or at least the top ten.

There are a lot of lessons here. I must remember that when God is at work in my life and my heart is tender toward the Holy Spirit, Satan will work to counterfeit God's work in me or he will try to sabotage it.

The good news is that just as the best time to transplant is after the rain because the ground is soft and it is easier to remove the plant, the best time to resist Satan's counterfeit is when God's Holy Spirit is working in your heart and you are yielding to Him. The longer you wait to let the Holy Spirit work and reveal things in your life, the harder the ground of your heart becomes, and the same is true of the weeds you allow to grow. They are harder to pull out, and sometimes when the ground is too hard, you don't get the whole weed, so you may leave part of the root. Weeds can grow from roots. It will come back, and you will have to deal with it again.

Another thing I noticed about the beetle attack was the timing. The beetles did not come to devour my plants until the fruit was ripe. What a warning this is to us. It was only the plants with ripe fruit or lush leaves that the beetles wanted to feed on. It is the same way in God's kingdom; Satan probably will not attack a life that is not a threat to his kingdom. He wants what is God's, and he cannot stand for a believer to love the Lord Jesus and live a life in love with Him. The Bible tells us that Satan comes to rob, kill, and destroy (see John 10:10). Sound familiar?

I'm not saying the beetles were Satan; I am saying that there are lessons we can learn from the order of nature that our Heavenly Father has created. There is no Mother Nature or Father Nature. There is Almighty God, creator of heaven and earth, and we are to worship Him and love and obey Him with all our hearts, which is the first commandment. He has made a way of salvation through faith in the blood of Jesus Christ and forgiveness for our sin, and He has given us His Holy Spirit to dwell in us and give the power to resist evil and live for Him.

I am amazed by God's love for me and His awesome beauty and power.

# 14

MARRIAGE

*Sunday, August 20, 2006*

A few days ago, I noticed a maple sapling that my husband and I had planted. It had been rescued from our garden. We already have two beautiful maples that we planted two and three years ago. New ones sprout up in the garden or among the berry bushes, and after they are a foot or so high, it is so hard to just pull them out and toss them, so we plant them. One of the trees that we rescued from the blackberry bush about three years ago is beautiful. It is eight to ten feet tall and has a great shape to it thanks to Mitch's pruning. There is a life lesson there.

This particular sapling, I noticed, we had planted together. Our other trees we planted separately: Mitch planted one, and I planted the other. I am very sentimental, so I called this "our tree." It is important to me because it is something that we did together. Now you would think that after more than twenty-six years of marriage, we would have done a lot of things together. We have. But we also have built our own lives and identities separately. That is only natural. Mitch is our provider and works outside our home, and I am a stay-at-home wife and mother. We (I) have home schooled our daughter from first through twelfth grade. We have parented together, built our home together (not literally), and established our family. But now our daughter has graduated from high school and begun her life as a young adult, establishing herself. Mitch and I now must regroup and build our marriage as a couple, around each other, not just around our parenting and family dynamics. Hence the maple sapling.

A few months ago, we attended an excellent weekend retreat for married couples. It was great. It has helped prepare us for this new transition. We realized again that our marriage relationship is the most important one that we have (next to our walk with the Lord), and we must nurture and cultivate it. So, we are looking for new ways to do things together.

This little sapling is actually two years old. It came up last year in our garden. Every time someone tilled the garden, I put something around the tree and made sure they saw it and left it alone. Well, this year was a great spring for trees. It was warm and very wet. This little sapling took off. I kept thinking that we had better get it transplanted, but it was also a busy spring for us, full of very difficult and stressful times. Transplanting a little tree was not high on the priority list; it wasn't even on the list. That is until after the weekend retreat. Then Mitch and I began looking for small, simple things that we could do together.

One afternoon, I asked Mitch if he would transplant this little tree. I had just the spot for it. He agreed, but it turned out to be a bigger job than he anticipated. It had a large taproot. That's why it shot up so quickly. In order to give it a good start in the new location, Mitch needed to dig deep and not damage the root. It took a while, but we (he) got the tree transplanted. We did it together (I helped).

Anyone who has ever transplanted something knows that the first thing something does when transplanted is to die. It doesn't really die; it goes into shock and drops its leaves to conserve its energy. That is what our little tree did. I kept telling Mitch that it would come out of it, but he was the one who had worked so hard to dig it out, and he wasn't sure. There was a point when I wasn't so sure either, and I was sorry I had called it our tree. Then I began seeing small green sprouts on the base of the trunk. I stripped all the leaves off to help it not struggle to drop them. Mitch then pruned it back (I think he has a ministry of pruning), and it started to come alive! As I looked at it, I realized it was able to make the transition from being dug up, relocating, losing its leaves, and being chopped back with pruning shears because of its strong taproot.

I saw such an analogy to our marriage. Mitch and I were both believers when we got married. We loved the Lord and were in Christian ministry in India and Europe for eleven years. We knew that the Lord had put our lives together, and we loved each other. That has not kept us from hard trials and painful seasons. But our taproot goes deep; it is our walks with the Lord and our commitment to our marriage. We have, by the grace of God, stayed faithful to our marriage.

Our tree didn't survive the next Illinois winter, but our marriage has with God's help. There are so many lessons we can learn from God's wonderful creation. And He has left us a manual to follow for our lives: His Word, the Bible. If we follow His instructions, we have a much better chance of making it through the winters of life.

Another thing I noticed this morning was that when I walked into the house, I left a trail of wet grass. I had been walking in the early morning while the dew was still on the grass. My shoes were covered with the morning's wet grass and leaves. As I walked through the kitchen, it left a trail. That is what happens when we walk in the early morning with Jesus. We will leave a trail. Those around us will see where we have been walking, that we have been with the Lord.

# 15

## HIDING PLACES

ஒ *August 11, 2006* ൲

It is a beautiful fall morning outside. The only problem is we are in the middle of summer! There shouldn't be autumn leaves all over the patio, but there are. I have looked at them for about a week now. I have asked everyone to please get the blower and clean off the patio. There has been one delay (or excuse) after another. This morning, I decided to do it myself. It is amazing what lessons there are in just a patio full of wet, dead leaves.

I found the blower; someone had borrowed it and it was not put back in the right place. It was out of gas: another delay. But I was determined to clean off the patio. Then I saw the bright yellow garage broom. Aha! I would do it the old-fashioned way. By hand.

As I started sweeping, it was so relaxing. I began moving the patio furniture around so I could sweep back into the corners and get the leaves that had gathered there. I thought about my own life, how when the Lord begins cleaning in my heart, He gets way back in the corners. He uncovers all my hiding places.

Sweeping is very thorough; it is deliberate. The more you do it, the better you are at it.

It's not that I am not used to sweeping or working—I am. I love to keep our home clean and welcoming. But I usually leave the outside mowing and yard work to my husband and our daughter, who helps him. Today, my husband was at work, and our daughter had moved into her first apartment last weekend. So, I am on my own. Our daughter, Elisabeth, who is such a sweetheart, moved closer to her work last week. Her dad and I are adjusting to our *empty nest*. I think the phrase should be the *vacuum in our heart*. The phrase empty nest just doesn't seem to paint the full picture.

I realize now that my story is not about some dead leaves, but about what God is doing in my heart as I adjust to this new phase in my life. When Elisabeth was born more than eighteen years ago, my life changed forever. Last weekend when she officially started her life on her own, she changed my life again, forever. After Elisabeth was born, things were so different that I lovingly referred to life before she was born as B.E. (Before Elisabeth). Now I guess it will be A.E.: yep, After Elisabeth.

It's not that Elisabeth is the center of my world; Jesus is. I know that for certain, but ever since I can remember, all I wanted to be was a wife and mother. God has given me the desires of my heart. I married the man I wanted to (we were friends for seven years before he asked me—yes, I have questioned him about the wait!), and the Lord gave us a beautiful, healthy daughter that lived.

We had two daughters who died at birth, Amy Eleanor, who was born on January 4, 1985, and died three hours and twenty minutes later on January 5, 1985. She was born in Peshawar, Pakistan, where my husband and I were missionaries.

Our second daughter, Kathryn Ruth, was born on September 16, 1986; she lived just a few minutes. She would have been twenty years old in about five weeks.

So maybe that will help explain why it was so difficult to see Elisabeth move out on her own. I have had more than nineteen years of being a mom. I will always be her mom, but it won't be the same. That's God's order. As her mother, I have taught her and trained her to grow into a mature, godly woman. Now the hard part comes as I must step back and let that happen.

It seems like God has been speaking to my heart in almost everything I do. He's teaching me how to let go, what I am to do now (pray), and that He is not finished with me. Thank you, Lord!

Everyone who knows me well knows how difficult this is, and in very subtle ways—some not so subtle (my husband keeps putting a book about empty nesters, with a certain chapter that he would like for me to read in front of me); it's his way of trying to help me.

Some encourage me to keep busy. That is never a problem in canning season! Others are sharing how they handled letting go of their oldest child. It all helps. God uses each kind word or action to let me see He is in control. He is my loving Heavenly Father, He formed our daughter in the womb, and He has a plan for her that is perfect for her. I will wait and see it unfold and bathe her in prayer.

The Lord is good to me. He speaks to me in ways that I understand, even in some wet, dead leaves.

SECTION

# TWO

❧ *More Life Lessons* ☙

# 16

## MORE LIFE LESSONS

*ℬ September 27, 2006 ℛ*

I have just finished putting together all the stories that I have written over the last seven years or so into a book. I have actually written more, but I have lost track of them, never thinking I would ever do anything with them. I have found that when the Lord is working in my life, it helps me make sense of things better when I write about it to myself, so to speak. So, a few years ago, I started writing down these life lessons.

I ran into a problem immediately. I walked outside, and the Lord began speaking to my heart about the things I saw and what I was doing. I thought, "I can't keep writing this down because I have already finished the book."

I had just put all the writings into a book, and I didn't think I could add another lesson to it. But I could because this is for me. It helps me make sense of what the Lord is doing in my life. It is my journal. I am writing this for myself so that I can go back and see all that the Lord is working in my life.

This brings me to this morning. I was reading in Nehemiah 13. The last recorded words we have of Nehemiah are "Remember me, O my God, for good" (v 31). If you stopped there and never said another word, that would be sufficient. That is my prayer for me; it's not original, but it says it all. My Bible bookmark that marks this place in my Bible has Psalm 46:10 on it: "Be still, and know that I am God." Wow!

This is what God is doing in my life.

He is making me be still.

Our good car broke down last week. We literally had prayed our way home a few times. We always had made it. Last week, when I came out of the post office—it's only three blocks from home—it was different. The first thing was it wouldn't start. I prayed. After the third time, the engine turned over, I think literally. A huge cloud of white smoke billowed out of the exhaust and blocked my rear-view window, but it was the loud banging noise coupled with the smell of burning oil that scared me.

I thought, "It's only three blocks home; I can make it." I started rolling. I didn't stop for the two stop signs. I was afraid that if I stopped, I wouldn't get the car to start again, so I rolled through them. We call it the *California roll*. I wonder if they call it the *Illinois roll* in California. It was a sight; people actually came out of their houses to see where the noise was coming from. When I pulled (glided) into our drive, the noise woke my husband, who was napping on the couch. He came running out of the house asking me if that was our car. I said yes. I landed safely, but the car has not started since.

I find myself still.

I literally cannot go anywhere. I have been praying about a lot of things. They are good things: what I would like to do, where I need to go. I want to be about my Heavenly Father's business. But I can't. I don't have a car (that moves). I have been getting frustrated. So, this morning when I was reading in Nehemiah, I realized that God was answering prayer.

I was right where He wanted me.

In all my busyness, I wasn't being still so that I could know Him. So, in His great and tender love for me, He stopped me from my activity so that I could still my heart and listen to Him. He was remembering me for good.

I love the Lord! He is so good to me. I know in His time; He will provide what I need. And when He has done the work He wants in my life, I will again be about my Father's business.

You see, who I am and how I have let God work in my life are more important than what I do, even if it is good that I do.

God is concerned with the vessel. He can fill it or use it as He plans, but if our vessel is unusable, He won't fill it. He will not pour His Holy Spirit into an unclean vessel. That is why we must continually come to Him in prayer and ask Him to search our hearts and minds and cleanse us with the powerful, precious blood of His Son, Jesus Christ. Psalm 51:10 says, "Create in me a clean heart, O God; and renew a right spirit within me."

King David of Israel wrote that, and the Bible says he was a man after God's own heart. How much more should I ask God to do the same work in my life?

He will.

He is.

He is faithful.

# 17

# MOTHERHOOD: A LEGACY OF LOVE

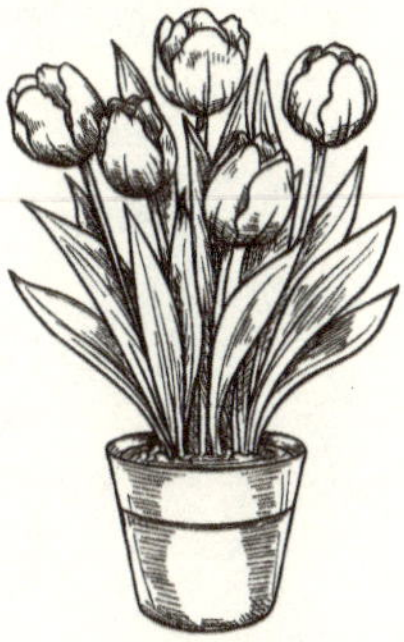

*October 2006*

If we are only able to leave behind the good that we do, our influence will be very limited. But if we leave behind our ideals and goals through our children, then we have affected the future. Motherhood is powerful. It is my greatest joy. I take this example from my mother. My mother, Shirley, was from a large family and lost her own mother to death in childbirth when she was six years old. I think that had a great impact on her.

My mom molded my life. One of the greatest things she did was to let me be who God created me to be. My mother was, for most of my life, a stay-at-home mom, but she was also a doctor's assistant, a dental assistant, and a chiropractic assistant as well as an excellent cook and homemaker. She worked late into the night each day. (I thought it was normal to go to sleep with the sound of the vacuum going.)

I asked her once what she would have done if she had not married and had me and my brother, Carl. She said she would probably have been a brain surgeon. I think she would have.

But the greatest influence my mother left me was her kind and selfless spirit. No one ever entered our home without being served. No one ever left hungry. And I never remember hearing my mother speak evil about one person. She was kind and giving, and when I would get upset because I felt someone was taking advantage of her, she put me in my place.

No, she was not perfect. But as she lay dying of cancer, she left me her greatest legacy: she met a painful death with peace in her faith. At her funeral procession, the cars stretched for miles. People that she had served in her life with kindness and respect now came to honor her memory and give me her last gift: an honorable legacy.

Now I am teaching my daughter those same values. My mother's influence continues on. Thank you for letting me share this legacy with you.

# 18

## SOME THOUGHTS
## ON WINTER WATERING

*♘ November 24, 2006 ♞*

This morning as I was cleaning up and watering the flowers on my counter, I was reminded that I needed to water the two beautiful plants that I had brought in for the winter. They are house plants, but each spring, I set them outside for our too-short summer. They thrive. It is amazing to see these two average plants explode with vibrant color and lush growth.

There are very logical reasons for this, scientific ones also, but I don't think I could articulate them to their credit. So, I will keep it simple for my sake. First, the early spring and summer bring such increased natural light. So, I put them outside in the light. If I left them inside, this extra light would not do them any good. And the warmth of summer signals for the growth hormones to wake up from their dormant winter sleep. So, I move them around. I change things so they can receive the maximum good from the summer warmth and light.

Then at some point in the fall, before the frost, I bring them in. I need to protect them from our cold Illinois winter. The plants always go through a shock. There is less natural light, and because they are in another part of the house, they get less water. They always survive, but the plants do not look as beautiful and lush as they do with the optimum conditions.

This morning as I watered the two plants, I was amazed at the changes only a few weeks indoors had made. One of the plants, called a spider or airplane, was struggling. About one-third of the leaves had already died off, and the shoots were limp and scraggly. It doesn't matter, though: I will keep watering and feeding it through the winter until spring comes and I can set it outside to grow and bring beauty to our porch again.

The other plant, a purple variegated vine, wasn't doing too badly. In fact, it seemed like bringing it inside was good for it. Some of the leaves had died, but the beautiful purple had turned a deep green. It was like the colors reversed. In the bright light, purple was dominant;

inside with minimum light, the green deepened. It had adjusted. It used the change to its advantage. It continued to thrive despite the changes.

As I looked at the plants, I thought about these lessons. I brought my plants in to protect them from the hard winter I knew was coming. The Lord does that for us. He knows what is coming, and He always moves on our behalf to protect us. Many times, He will bring changes to do that. I don't know about others, but change is almost always difficult for me. I work very hard at getting things the way I want them, and then when there is change, I have to start all over again! But my loving Heavenly Father knows me so well, and He knows that change is good for me.

In gardening, there is a term *root bound*. The picture of it is when a flower is planted in a pot, and it has grown and grown and grown ... and then seems to stop. If you take that plant and turn it upside down and gently pull it from its pot, you will see that the root has filled the pot. There was nowhere else to go, and so the growth was stopped. Growth only comes from the root. So that is when you go and buy a bigger pot and transplant. The size of the new pot is determined by the amount of growth you expect.

That is what God does. He sees that we (I) become root bound. I need more room to grow. Then He changes something in my life. Sometimes it is an easy thing, sometimes not. Sometimes it is deep and only He knows how deep the pot needs to be to support the growth that He is expecting in my life.

Just as the two plants reacted differently to the changes, we can too. We can resist the new things that God has brought and fight against them, using our energy for the fight. Or we can adjust and let the new change bring out the best in us.

Winter is a time of rest. Nature lies dormant on the surface. God allows winter in our lives for a reason. It is a signal for rest, to prepare us for the new growth that will come in the spring.

Winters in Illinois do not last forever. In fact, they probably do not last even as long as we think they do. They just seem to last forever until spring comes, and then we will forget the shortened hours of sunlight, the bitter cold winds, and the barrenness of the landscape.

Our Heavenly Father created each season. He will not let the winter in your life last longer than is necessary. It would defeat His purpose. There will always be spring. Then our loving Heavenly Father will carry us into His Son's light for a season of growth.

# 19

## FINDING REAL TREASURE

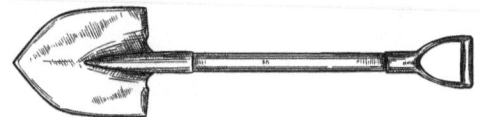

*ஐ December 10, 2006 ை*

I wasn't feeling well this morning. I have been fighting the flu. I could feel my body telling me to take precautions, like drinking more water, taking extra vitamins, etc. Last week when I was out, almost everyone had a story about the flu. This morning at about 3, I had to get up because I was sick. I was hoping that I would feel better in time to go to church, but I didn't, so my husband went on and he said they would miss me in the Sunday school class he teaches.

I finally felt a little better and decided to get up and get a cup of hot tea and a soft blanket and snuggle up in a big chair and read. So, I grabbed my *Prayers That Avail Much*, by Germaine Copeland and Andrew Murray's *Humility & Absolute Surrender* and started for the chair, but I realized I didn't have my Bible. I went to get it and picked up the zipped cover for it. All my pens and note papers fell out. So, I took a minute to clean out the things that I had stuffed into the cover.

That's when I found the money. Two $5 bills, tucked in my Bible cover. I got a little excited. It's always nice to reach into your pocket and find some money you didn't know was there; it's like finding some hidden treasures.

Just then, the Lord spoke to my heart and told me that the real treasure lay in His Word. I did not find the money (treasure) until I went to get my Bible. I had to put things in order before I could find the money that at some point I had tucked into the zipper. The money was there all the time, but I didn't find it until I was cleaning out some stuff that was hiding it.

It is like that in our lives; sometimes stuff hides God's treasures from us. And it is like that when reading our Bibles; we have to search and look into the corners, so to speak, many times to find His treasure. Jeremiah 33:3 says: "Call unto Me, and I will answer thee, and shew thee great and mighty [translated *hidden* in the English Standard Version things, which thou knowest not."

Yes, the other books and devotionals that I read encourage and minister to my heart, but only His Word is alive and quick and powerful. I'm sure that the two books I had picked up had started with the writers finding their real treasures in His Word, and they were passing on some of it to us. But I must never forget what the source of real treasure is: my Heavenly Father.

So, I will take my Bible and the other things, and I will look for some hidden treasure.

# 20

## FIRST FROST

*ᔓ January 2, 2007 ᔕ*

It is hard to believe that it is 2007 already, January 2. As I looked out this morning, I saw that we had a hard frost overnight, the first of 2007. It was beautiful! Everything was covered with sparkling crystals. I walked back into the kitchen a little bit later and noticed that the frost was burning off with the sun coming up. You could once again see the green grass except for the places that were shadowed: where the shed was, the garage, the fence. In those places, the hard frost was still in place. You could see it so clearly, like it was a coloring picture.

I saw a bigger meaning there. Winter is a season. You expect hard winter storms; they bring snow, frost, and sometimes bitter cold. It wasn't unusual to wake up and see frost, and it's normal for the sun's warmth to melt it. Our life seasons are like that.

Winter will come to Illinois every year. Fact.

Winters will come to a believer's life sometimes. Fact.

Every house in my hometown had frost on the ground. I wasn't singled out, and as believers, winters will come to each of us. This morning, the areas that were not in direct sunlight melted slowly. In our lives as Christians, areas where we do not let the sunlight of the Holy Spirit work will stay in winter frost longer.

I want the Son's light in my life to warm the areas of my life and heart that have known the hard frosts of winter.

So, I will yield my life to Jesus daily, seeking Him in prayer and asking the Holy Spirit to show anything that might be shadowing His warmth from reaching me, as I commit this new year to Him.

# 21

## A WORD ABOUT SNOW

&❧ *February 10, 2007* ❧&

We had a beautiful snow the other day. It was about three inches, just enough to cover the brown spots in the yard, the twigs that had dropped over the winter, the fall plants that were left until spring to prune back, and the gray that seems to settle over the landscape.

The beauty of new fallen snow is comparable to the mountains or the ocean. But there is something about new snow, bright, white, and sparkling ...it is so special. Maybe it is because it is not always there. It's a surprise event; you wake up and look out your window—and wow! It is a beautiful sight. It is not easily forgotten. It covers everything, like a pure white blanket making everything it covers look so clean.

I wonder if that is why God used this word picture to show us how His love for us can cover our sins. Isaiah 1:18 says, "Though your sins be as scarlet [my addition: bright red, out there for everyone to see, impossible not to notice], they shall be as white as snow." If you have never seen fresh snow up close and personal: well, a picture may be worth a thousand words, but snow has a feel to it, a fresh clean smell, and a coldness. You KNOW when you have touched it.

That is the difference between seeing it in a picture and experiencing it in person. I think there are many who have a picture kind of relationship with Jesus. You have seen the pictures; you may even go to church. But your sins have not been blotted out by trusting in the atoning blood of the Lord Jesus Christ.

Jesus covers our sins and makes them as snow. Just as the snow covers all the ugly scars and debris of the winter, the Bible says the blood of the Lord covers our sins and makes us white as snow. Romans 10:9 says, "If thou shalt confess with thy mouth the Lord Jesus, and shalt believe in thine heart that God hath raised him from the dead, thou shalt be saved." And His blood will cleanse us from all unrighteousness.

If you do not know this One who can cleanse your heart and make you white as snow, open your heart to Him today.

# 22

## A HARD LESSON

*April 30, 2007*

I can hardly believe that it is almost May 1. The grass is finally turning green, and the trees are starting to leaf out. This actually happened around April 1; it looked like it was going to be an early spring, but just as the buds were budding and leaves were leafing, we had a cold snap—actually two of them—and whatever was sprouting died in its tracks.

That happens. But this year, it was a cold blast that hit 19 degrees. This cold snap did more than make us turn on the furnace again; it killed trees and flowers. They won't be coming up as the sun shines and the weather warms up. It was something.

What was different about this? We have cold, freezing weather all winter, and plants survive. This was different because the plants had come out of hibernation, their juices had started to flow, and they were growing. Because they were in the growth stage, the cold weather killed them. Wow.

I began to think about people, especially young people. How important that tender growing stage is for them. Sometimes as parents, adults, or Sunday school teachers, we forget that the growing stage is different from other stages of life. We have to be so careful that while instructing we don't kill the young life that has been entrusted to us.

Maybe that is why many young people have left the church: when they were at a tender growing stage, someone killed their faith or at least damaged it.

As older believers, we have a responsibility to pray for and nurture the young that God has entrusted to our care.

# 23

THANK YOU, LORD

ℰ෨ *May 19, 2007* ෬ℛ

I love order, neatness, a clean house, the Lord, my family, and flowers. Not in that order ... I see God's handiwork in His creation. The beauty and creativeness in flowers alone are unsurpassed (except for His finest creations: men and women).

We have a lot of flowers around our home. Some are perennials: they come up every year (sometimes). The rest are annuals, and they must be bought and planted every year. I find great joy and satisfaction in growing flowers. A beautiful rose bush can take an old fence that has broken places in it and totally transform it for the months out of the year that it is in bloom.

Many times, God has used His creation to speak to me and show me His character and His work in my life. It never ceases to amaze me that at the most unexpected times, God will speak to my heart from His order—nature—and it never grows old. He has set the stars in the heavens and given us the sun to give light by day, the moon to give light to the night, and the seasons to order our times.

Flowers are beautiful, but they are alive and therefore they need water and nourishment. So, I spend a lot of time fertilizing and watering. Fertilizing is bi-monthly, but watering is daily, or as often as it needs to be. It takes a lot of time and commitment. In early spring, it is usually not so difficult to find or make the time to water, but as the months pass, my time gets tighter.

This Saturday morning was one of those times. I needed to leave early, and I had a list of things that needed to be done before I left. I had been busy the day before also and only finished half of the watering. I am thankful for the blessing of having beautiful flowers at our home; it would be ungrateful not to take good care of them. So, I went out very early and watered.

I was on my way back—I have a route I take when I water or else I leave some area out—when I saw this beautiful yellow plant, When I looked closer, I saw it was covered with tiny yellow daisy-like flowers. It was beautiful. I felt like the Lord told me it was there for me to find. It was on the shaded side of the house under a larger flower. It shouldn't have been able to grow there, but it did. A bird had dropped a seed and it sprouted, and because I was being faithful to care for the beautiful things the Lord had allowed me to have, I found it. I took it and transplanted it where it would get the best sunlight and it would fill the flower bed with beautiful yellow blooms.

There are a lot of lessons here for me. I wonder if you can see some in your own life. God is always speaking. I have never seen Him face-to-face—I think only Moses has—but He has given us His Word, the Bible, and His witness in creation. Psalm 19 says that the heavens declare (or shout) His glory. Those who have been born again (see John 3:1-5) know Him and we are His witnesses of His work in our lives. I am a witness of His work in my life. Thank you, Lord!

# 24

## THE EYE OF THE STORM

* හ July 28, 2007 ඓ*

I have heard that when the weather planes fly out to sea during a hurricane, they encounter something called the eye of the storm. It means that they are flying through total calm, peace in the midst of a hurricane.

This morning as I was praying, I realized that I was flying in the eye of the storm. When I came into the presence of my Heavenly Father, I was enveloped with such peace that can only be explained as the presence of God. I was in the eye of my storm.

The Lord gave me such a picture of this: Outside of the eye is destruction. It is said that most of the damage done during a hurricane is not from the wind itself but from the flying debris.

I am experiencing a hurricane. In almost every corner of my life, things are happening that are very important and which I have little or no control over. I see people I love being challenged, hurt, and groping for answers, and I am unable to help. Some of these things are happening to me. I am going through one of the most difficult times in my life. I have walked down this path before, but I have not gone this deep into the woods. This is unfamiliar territory, and I don't think I am doing well.

I don't usually write like this. I look forward to the times when the Lord will speak to my heart and I write these insights or life lessons down so that I will remember them, but this is the first time that I have felt the Lord impress upon my heart to write now, in the midst of my storm, so to speak.

I have been praying that God would work into my life Proverbs 31:26: "She openeth her mouth with wisdom; and in her tongue is the law of kindness." That is my heart's desire. That doesn't seem to be what is happening. Several times lately, what I thought was said as true and honest has been mistaken as something totally different. And in some cases, I did not speak the whole truth because I thought it was best and it brought terrible consequences. This is not my hurricane; this is just some of the debris. But ...

This is what God used that morning to speak His truth to my heart and put me in the eye of the storm, His place of peace and rest. God used His Word to tell me He wanted truth in the inward part, the whole truth. He hates lies and deceit; even half-truths are lies. The Lord lets the Holy Spirit be the candle to light up the darkness that is in the inner man, me. Imagine that: I am praying for all these situations around me (that is a good thing), and God wants to work in me to answer my prayers that I would open my mouth with wisdom and on my tongue would be the law of His kindness. How can I carry these burdens and still let God refine me without being crushed by the debris? I find the eye of the storm, His presence and rest, because the Lord told me that His yoke is easy and His burden is light.

I know that if the Lord is showing me things that He will also do them. That is the hope I have been looking for, a word from Him, that He is in control when things around me look out of control. I know there are those who have been to this place I am at; they are the great cloud of witnesses that the book of Hebrews speaks about. They experienced God's faithfulness through their hurricane. I can too.

You may be experiencing a hurricane in your life. Maybe it seems like just a tropical storm, but it doesn't take much to be upgraded to a hurricane. Your circumstances might be different, but the answer is the same. TRUST. Proverbs 3:5-6 says, "Trust in the Lord with all thine heart; and lean [or trust] not unto thine own understanding. In all thy ways [thoughts, words, actions] acknowledge him, and he shall direct thy paths."

# 25

## CLEANING IN AN ICE STORM

*December 9, 2007*

We are in the middle of an ice storm. There is not a whole lot to do in circumstances such as this, so I decided to do some cleaning in our bedroom. I have been busy lately, and so a few things have piled up. This is also Christmastime, and I have a few piles of things lying around.

That drives me crazy. To put it gently, I would say I am a clean nut. I love to organize and clean, and I love it when everything is organized and clean. That means that I usually have a very clean house or a very messy house. The downside of being a clean nut (besides driving those around me a bit nuts) is that if I am not careful, I find my fulfillment and some identity in my cleaning and organization.

There is a Scripture that says that a dish of vegetables where there is love is better than a fatted calf where there is strife (see Proverbs 15:17). In paraphrase, it means it is better to have the beds unmade and dishes in the sink, but when your husband or daughter walk in the door, they feel that you missed them and are so glad they are home. Compare that to having a beautiful meal on the table and the house is spotless, but when your husband and daughter walk in the door, they feel that they have intruded into your world of order and clean and they can stay here, but they must pick up *afterthemselves* (all one word!). (My daughter just told me that a beautiful meal is nice either way. She is a sweetie!)

I can speak from both experiences. The fatted calf and strife are not the answer; the situation is not what it is cracked up to be. It is exceedingly better to value those of value and let them know that than to live your life in a world of perfection (which is just an illusion) by yourself.

In my cleaning, I had the latest, easiest gadget: a duster with a spray attachment. I like it. It is easy and convenient, and I dust till I run out of spray, which is an incentive. It works for me. Well, today I was using my one spray on everything. That worked fine until I dusted a gift that was more than thirty-five years old, a music box from my high school best friend.

I noticed immediately that the spray was causing the top to peel. Ahh! So, I stopped, and it made me think that friendships and relationships are like that: Many times, we try to use the same ideas or techniques on each person in our life. It usually doesn't work. Each person is a gift. They have value and are unique. We should take the time to invest in understanding that to the fullest. It may not fit into our normal way of doing things, but I don't think anyone will be disappointed with the outcome.

# 26

## SPRING FLOWERS

ℰℴ *April 7, 2008* ℘ℬ

I was just outside; it is finally a beautiful spring day! And as I was looking for the spring flowers in our yard, I came across this scene. In one of the (many) flower beds in our yard, I saw a flower—still just the green leaves—pushing its way up through the winter mulch (and the natural mulch that the dying leaves leave behind). I know this flower; I planted it. It is a pretty pink flower that is very fragrant, but if someone didn't know what I know, they would wonder what this was.

This flower (leaf) is covered in leaves, dirt, and mulch, yet it is pushing its way up so that it can grow and give the beauty it was created to give. You can almost see the struggle it goes through, breaking through the hard earth.

I think this is a picture of life.

First, it is the One who created us (planted us) who knows us best. Even when others cannot recognize who we are, or the beauty in our lives, He does.

Second, life is hard, like the ground, but God has equipped us to push through. It's amazing how a fragile plant can break through the hard earth and yet its tender leaves are not damaged. Sometimes I wonder how the difficult things in life will not harden me or crush me, but they don't. I think that is because God intended for those things to strengthen and mold us, not crush us, and if we push through, the world will see the beauty and know the fragrance (kindness, thoughtfulness, mercy) that our lives give out.

I hope this will be an encouragement for you today.

# 27

## KATH'S FLOWERS

ର *August 29, 2008* ଔ

It is a beautiful Las Vegas (Boulder City) morning! I am visiting a dear friend who celebrated a milestone birthday this year. The Lord was gracious and allowed me to find a $26.98 plane ticket to come and see her! I wanted to make the visit special for her because I knew she would make it very special for me. So, I had a bouquet of fresh flowers sent to her on the morning I was to arrive with a card saying, "See you later!"

Kath loves to send flowers to people to make them feel special. She sent my husband and me a beautiful planter for our twenty-fifth wedding anniversary. It was such a blessing that I tucked away the hope that someday I would be able to return the favor. This was it! I was so excited to get to see the bouquet that had come. It is beautiful, full of lavender daisies, carnations, baby's breath, and a beautiful single pink rose. The florist had done an excellent job.

I have been here for a week now, and every day I notice the vase of flowers once or twice a day. I love it. This morning as I was coming in from my quiet time with the Lord, I noticed the vase again. It was the first time this morning, although I had passed it several times already. I felt the Lord speak to my heart: that is what happens many times throughout my day. God has set something in my path to bless me, but I just don't take the time to notice the beauty and blessing that have been sent just for me!

There really is something to the old adage "Stop and smell the roses."

# 28

## SOME THOUGHTS ON ZERO

ഇ *November 16, 2008* ര

"It was a big zero!" I am sure that we all have heard that phrase in reference to something; I know I have. But this morning, I thought about how people are sometimes referred to as a zero, a nothing. But is that really accurate? Actually, a zero can be very valuable, especially in the life of an individual. We may look at someone and think, Is there anything special about that person or anything of great value? But the better question is, how does God view them? His Word is very clear how He sees each of us as precious.

As I was thinking about this, I thought of the value of zero. If it were possible (just go with me here for a minute) to hand you a zero, what would you think? What would you do with it? Alone, the zero has little or no value, but combined with something else, the little zero can increase the value of what you are holding. For example: If I give you a blank check and write a five on it, you may say, "Thank you." A five is greater than a zero, but alone, it really is of little worth, right? Imagine I then hand you a zero to add to that five. Oh, all of a sudden, your 5 becomes a 50, a little more valuable, correct? Let's go a little further and say I have a pocketful of zeros. I can see the smile on your face. Now your blank check with the five has the potential to become very valuable with each zero I give you.

I think life is like that. We are all like the five: alone we have value, but God in His infinite love and mercy is holding a pocketful of zeros for us. These are the life situations that are difficult or painful, or perhaps there are certain people that God has or will bring into your life to give it value.

I volunteer at a Christian radio station once a week. The station manager is totally blind. He is a most amazing man. He was born of rape (maybe some even think he ought to have been aborted) and labeled unadoptable because of the birth defects that were visible at birth. He was abandoned and abused as a young child. Not really the type of person that you would expect to succeed, don't you think? Yet that young man has graduated from college, holds a master's degree, is a pastor, owns his own home, lives alone (without a guide dog!), is a great cook, has computer skills that almost cause me to envy, and manages a radio station. That is only the outside. He visits nursing homes and encourages those less fortunate. Oh, and did I mention that he has a beautiful voice and has recorded three albums and many of his songs have been number one on the top one hundred played on the station? He is loved by everyone who knows him. At first glance, many might call him a zero ... but not God.

My life has been full of zeros, situations where I wondered what good could come of this or precious people that others may not feel have much value, but in reality, they are very important in our lives. Romans 8:28 says, "All things work together for good to them that love God, to them who are the called according to his purpose."

God has allowed that truth of His Word to work deep in my heart.

My first memory of that promise was in the fall of 1984. My husband and I were missionaries in Peshawar, Pakistan. I was in my first trimester of pregnancy. It was my second pregnancy; I had miscarried a year and half earlier while we were working in Colombo, Sri Lanka.

On this particular day, I had just come from the doctor who had ordered me to complete bed rest for two weeks. I was walking to our room and suddenly that Scripture filled my mind so clearly.

I wondered what it meant.

I was to learn.

Our daughter, Amy Eleanor, was born three months prematurely. And although I too was a three-month premature baby, our daughter only lived three hours and twenty minutes, and then the Lord dispatched His angels to bring her home.

Over the next many, many years, almost twenty-four now, I would see how God, my loving Heavenly Father, would cause the most painful hurt and loss I had ever known to be used for good in my life.

My life has been full of zeros that have become pluses and have added great value to my life. And for this I am thankful.

# 29

## A FLY IN THE KITCHEN

ജ *October 11, 2008* ൭

It is a beautiful, cold fall morning. I love mornings like this. I get up and the house is quiet, and I have a cup of hot tea and read my Bible. I need the quiet before the day really gets started.

I have been canning. This morning, I was cleaning up from the last batch of applesauce. I use a big roaster oven and let the apples cook overnight and then can them. This frees up my stove, but it leaves a mess in my roaster. Because the apples bake in the roaster, it bakes a hard crust that takes lots of elbow grease and just plain hard scrubbing to get off.

Today I am going to put on another batch of apples, so I was cleaning the hard crust off the roaster when I saw a fly in the kitchen. I grabbed my trusty flyswatter and took aim, fired, and missed! I turned to put the flyswatter away, thinking I would get him later. After all, it was only one fly, and when you are canning, they usually come in tribes!

As I turned, I felt the Lord speak to my heart that that is what we do with sin many times. Maybe there have been seasons in our lives when we were swarmed with many struggles that could cause us to sin, but because we saw it as only one, we put our flyswatter away thinking we would get it later.

I will go back and kill the fly before I begin canning. I don't want flies—single or plural—in my kitchen when I am cooking. I will also, by God's grace, not put away the flyswatter of my heart and not allow a single sin to trip me up. The Bible tells us it is the little foxes that spoil the vine (Song of Solomon 2:15). We must always be vigilant to guard our hearts. God promises us that if we commit our works to Him, our thoughts will be established (Proverbs 16:3). Thank you, Lord.

SECTION

# THREE

ↆ *Lessons in Everything* ↄ

# 30

## LESSONS FROM A WEE ONE

❧ *April 6, 2009* ☙

I just put our granddaughter to sleep. I am not sure how it happens that grandbabies and grandparents form such an intense bond of love immediately, but I know it happens. It happened with our daughter and my mom, and it has happened with me and our first granddaughter. It might be a spillover from the love we have for our children. How can we not love what is such a wonderful part of them?

Today our daughter and son-in-law had an errand to run, so they asked us if we would watch Michaela , who is fifteen months old, for them. They said she was ready for her afternoon nap. That always makes it go smoother! We have a portable crib set up in our guest room. It is quiet, warm, and upstairs away from household traffic.

We have a routine when I put her down for her nap. If I do any small thing differently, she doesn't go to sleep. I am not exactly sure how we developed such a routine, but we have. So today I took her upstairs and began rocking her. As I looked down at her face and kissed her, I realized that what I was doing was like my faith in the Lord.

She needed to rest; it is more difficult when I don't hold her until she relaxes. It seems like when I pick her up, she will go to sleep within minutes. I think it's because she senses I am not in a hurry. If I rush trying to get her to fall asleep, she won't. It is a matter of trust. She trusts that I will stay until she doesn't know I am there (asleep), so she relaxes. I wait until I see her eyes close …and stay closed, she stops taking her bottle, and then her breathing changes. It slows down and becomes very light and even.

I usually wait a few more minutes just to be sure; if I jump the gun, she wakes up, and it is much harder to get her back to sleep. Then after I am sure she is sound asleep; I have a difficult decision to make. Do I put her down and get to the rest of my housework, or do I just enjoy one of the sweetest moments a mom or grandmother can enjoy: to hold a sweet, precious, sleeping baby?

I see my loving Heavenly Father like that. He is not in a hurry. When I come to Him in prayer, He is waiting, patiently, to hear me out.

He waits until I come to a place of being able to express my heart, what is really on my heart. If I would come into His presence and feel as though He were just waiting until I was finished so He might go rescue someone else, I know that I would not be able to trust my heart to Him.

It is about trust—and I can learn it from a baby.

# 31

## LESSONS IN EVERYTHING

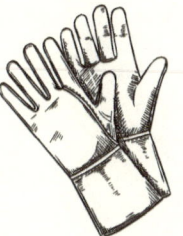

*May 2009*

I was just doing some mending.

I got a great deal on a casual skirt, so I bought three. But they are too long. The story of my life! So, I am mending. I am on the second one. Each one gets shorter. Hand sewing is an art. Really.

It is like a work of art to sew beautiful handwork.

There are rules to mending if you want to do it right.

You probably have heard it said, "Measure twice, cut once." Yep. Been there, done that, as my mother-in-law says! Well, it usually is true.

I think one of the keys to great mending is the prep. Know what you are planning to do, and get organized. If you don't know what you want, how can you do it? Before I could hem, I had to know the correct length. So, I had to get the right tools and measure.

Sounds simple. Then cut, pin, and hem. I was putting a lot of time and money (even though I got them on sale) into something. I wanted to do it right, do a good job.

Isn't life like that? If we don't have a goal, how can we go there? How will we get there, physically, mentally, emotionally? What/who will we need to help us? We will only get one chance to walk this journey we call life.

Measure twice, cut once.

There is a Scripture that says, "For me and my house, we will serve the Lord" (Joshua 24:15).

I can't think of a better measuring stick (or rule) to live by.

# 32

## JUST A FEW THOUGHTS

*⤫ Fall 2009 ⤬*

I was having my hot tea this morning (inside! It is too chilly out) and I was admiring the beauty of the geraniums on the deck. I noticed that one of them had some withered leaves. I know what that means: it is dry, needs water, needs refreshment.

That made me think about the body of Christ, our brothers and sisters in Christ: we need to be sensitive to their needs. Do I/we notice that they need refreshing? We don't wear leaves that get dry (anymore anyway!), but we need to be sensitive to their spirits. Do they need refreshing?

If they do, we can reach out and encourage them with a word or genuine kindness. I have needed that in my life—many times. It is so wonderful when the Lord sends someone to refresh my spirit, to be on the receiving end. It is even more wonderful to be on the giving end and know that you have helped make a difference in someone else's life for the better.

I also noticed our climbing rose bush. You cannot help but notice it; it is huge and lush. When did that happen? The rose bush is planted at the pond and climbs up a windmill. It is eight years old this year. It has the most fragrant peach baby roses on it. When it is in bloom, you can smell the fragrance from several feet away. It is a star rose.

It has weathered some strong winds, hard winters, Japanese beetles, and radical pruning. It has always put forth these fragrant flowers, but the plant had always been a bit spindly. What could have made such a dramatic change this year? Now it is growing wild … hum. Wow. Can I see an analogy to our spiritual lives? It was the pruning and the just right growing conditions that caused it to produce this year.

Our lives are like that. Our Heavenly Father knows what He has gifted us with in our lives, but it takes purposeful pruning. Trials. Not getting things our own way for a season. Sorrow. Perhaps even the death of a dream. But if we will yield to the hand of the Master, who knows just how far to cut to produce the best, one day our lives will produce the beauty that will show the world how real He is. His tender love will be revealed in us through our trust and obedience to His will for us. Thank you, Lord. I love you for pruning my life.

# 33

ANOTHER ANNIVERSARY

⋙ *May 20, 2012* ⋘

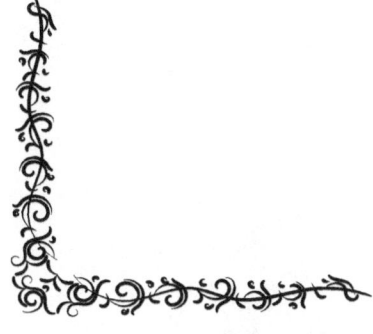

In eleven days, Mitch and I will celebrate our thirty-second anniversary. The last few years, I have felt like I have wanted to address this in a different way. On one hand, I declare that we made it, and I know it is by the grace of God. I celebrate, but I realize that though we have many friends who have been married twenty, thirty, forty, or more years, some of our dear friends' marriages have not survived the obstacle course or the battles that Satan has directed toward families.

Marriage is wonderful, but it is not easy. In fact, I think it is impossible without the Lord. Being married has brought me some of my most fulfilling moments: sharing the birth of Elisabeth and the birth of our granddaughter, Michaela. Mitch and I have experienced these times together.

Mitch and I also shared the common sorrow as we buried two little girls, his grandparents, two of his sisters, my mom, and his dad. We have traveled that road that changed as our life experiences have taken us from India to Illinois.

My marriage has also brought me some of the deepest heartache. I don't know why we expect two imperfect people to have a perfect marriage; it can't happen—in this life. It is true that opposites usually do attract and marry. Mitch and I are opposites. I think this is God-ordained to mold us into His image. He puts us into the deepest, most intimate relationship we can know and then begins to work to refine us. Many times, He uses the one person we desire to be the best for—our spouse—and begins to reveal those imperfections.

Mitch and I married for love. We were friends for seven years before he asked me to marry him. We didn't date. Mitch said when he knew he was ready to get married, I was the one he wanted to marry. He asked me. I told him I would pray about it! Three days later, he proposed on a rooftop in India. I said yes. We never held hands until we were engaged. He never kissed me until the day before our marriage (his idea, not mine!). You would think we would be setting sail for a blissful marriage, but this is NOT the reason our marriage has survived.

No. Our marriage has not been easy, but we have remained faithful to one another and, most importantly, to our faith in Christ. When our love was not holding us together, our commitment did. When one of us felt like giving up—thankfully, we never felt that way at the same time—one of us would be praying and holding on.

So, we have held on for thirty-two years on May 31, 2012. And I am writing this in gratefulness to the Lord who has helped us and kept us. My desire is to encourage our friends and acquaintances who for one or more reasons have found themselves unable to keep their marriage. It takes two. Not one. Two. For every divorce, there is a story. Each story is important, and from every hurt, there can/must be healing. Not just for those who have gone through a divorce: I am still married, but God has had to heal some very deep, painful hurts in our marriage. Some are mine, and some I have caused.

I think what I am trying to say is that in whatever place we find ourselves, it is grace, God's grace, that carries us through. I am so thankful that Mitch and I are still married. I love him. But I know it is not enough. It takes me loving Jesus first with all my heart and yielding my life to Him so that He is able to work His good will in my life. So, in whatever place you find yourself—married, divorced, or single— determine to love Jesus with all your heart because that is where the deepest love is found. As much as I love my family, there is a deep ache in my heart that can only be filled and completed as I know the Lord. We cannot put the expectation upon another to fill that deep need. We will be disappointed. God did not intend for any man or woman to take His place that He put in each of us. Only knowing and loving Him can do it.

# 34

PRAYER

❧ *Spring 2008* ❧

I would like to encourage you to pray.

I believe that prayer is one of the most important foundations of the Christian life. It is our lifeline to our Heavenly Father. If we don't pray, we are not communicating with our God. Our faith will stand still.

Prayer is based on faith. We have faith that the One we are talking to:

1. Is listening
2. Cares about what we are saying and will communicate back.

Faith is a big deal. The book of Hebrews says that "without faith it is impossible to please Him: for he that cometh to God must believe that he is, and that he is the rewarder [answerer] of them that diligently seek him" (11:6).

So, to pray, we must have faith.

How do we get that faith? I know in my life as I have sought to trust God, He has allowed me to take baby steps, so to speak. When I pray and see God answer, it builds my faith to believe more. When I hear someone share what God is doing in their life and how He answered prayer for them, that also helps build my faith.

I will never forget years ago in our adult Sunday school class, our teacher, Brother Bryant, stood up in front of the class one day and held up his keys.

He smiled as he shook them and said, "Do you see these? These are faith builders." (At this point, I began nudging Mitch, and I was smiling too; I knew what was coming!) He said, "If you knew how many times I have lost these and prayed to find them, you would understand."

I did understand because God had used the very same things in my life to build my faith. Oh, it wasn't always my house keys: sometimes it was money for the water bill or an important paper that had to be mailed yesterday. But each time I prayed that the Lord would help me find it, He did. To date, I do not have an outstanding account with the Lord.

Everything I have lost, misplaced, or forgotten where I put has been found. That is a lot of stuff over the years, let me tell you.

Two days ago, was the last "outstanding" thing I was looking for, which is why I am writing. It was the touch-up paint for our kitchen and living room. I keep touch-up jars of each color of each room we paint just in case we need them. Well, we needed them, and I couldn't find them anywhere. I turned the house upside down (not literally of course). I had put both jars in the kitchen and they had been there for months, but then we put a new floor in and everything was moved around for weeks. I had to find a new place for the paint where I could remember to find it. And I did. Find a new place, that is, but by the time we needed the jars for touch-ups, I had forgotten where they were. Well, it is not very nice to have a newly painted wall with white drywall mud spots showing. So, we were looking for paint. I prayed, and Mitch and I prayed, but I couldn't find them. A couple of weeks had gone by, and still, I couldn't find them.

Then the other night just before I was going to bed, I stopped and prayed again. I felt the Lord speak to my heart that the paint was on the top shelf of our barrister bookcase in the living room behind the books. I thought, "No." But then I remembered that when I had prayed before, I felt the same prompting, but then I said, "No, that can't be the Lord. I would never put paint behind the books in the living room. I would put it somewhere I would remember." So, this time, I quickly went into the living room and lifted up the glass door and reached behind the books on the top shelf, and guess what was there? You don't really have to guess. It was the paint.

You might say it was my subconscious—ha! I wish my subconscious was that on the ball, really. No, I did not remember putting it there. You see, this has happened to me so many times over the years that I do not question it; I know it comes from the Lord in answer to prayer.

I hope/pray that what I have shared will encourage you to pray and to have faith in our faithful Heavenly Father. He delights in us. Let us take delight in Him.

# 35

## MINING FOR GOLD

ഌ *Spring 2013* ര

I was thinking this morning that life is somewhat like being a miner for gold.

A gold miner's life was not easy. I have read very little on the subject, but I have watched a lot of Westerns, and their portrayal of this life shows it was not easy!

A gold miner would find a stake, perhaps a place near where someone had already found gold or somewhere he thought would hold the buried treasure. Then he would stake a claim on it, call it his, saying to everyone around that whatever treasure would be found on this land would be his and his alone.

Then he would begin the process of mining. If the gold was in the ground, he may have to use explosives to make a way for the hard work of digging that would follow. If the gold was in the streams that had washed the precious metal from the heart of the earth, he would pan for his treasure. And he would constantly be on alert for those who would try to steal his claim or the fruit of his labor.

I see life in the same way. We are all miners and life is hard. You have to be committed to find the gold. Just as real gold is buried deep in the heart of the earth, the real treasures of life are buried deep, and only those who are willing to mine (work for it) will enjoy its reward.

What are the treasures of life? I am sure each person would have their own to share, but some I feel are universal are: a happy home life, a good marriage, good family relationships, healthy children, financial security, and—most importantly—knowing how important we are to the One who created us.

Just as a miner might look to stake his claim in places where others have already found gold, we may tend to look to others who have found the things in life we think will make us happy. But unless we look in the right places, we are sure to be disappointed.

Our Heavenly Father has left us with a miner's guide, if you will; it is the Word of God, the Bible. That is the place where we will find buried treasure. We will find the wisdom and guidance we need to find the buried treasures of life. It will guide our decisions; teach us how to live peaceably with all men; and how to be the best parents, wives, and husbands we can be. That does not mean that life will be a bed of roses for us or that everything will turn out the way we want. I am sure there were hundreds, if not thousands, who went looking for gold but returned empty handed. But if we follow the Book and obey its guidelines, our lives will be richer no matter the outcome.

Life is not for cowards. It is hard work, and discouragements will come, but remember there are gold nuggets to be found along the way if you keep at it. I pray the Lord would bless you in your journey and draw your heart to Him, the true source of happiness.

# 36

## DARK MORNING

ᔐ *Spring 2014* ᔑ

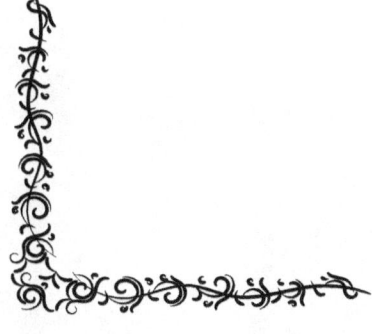

I was sitting outside this morning enjoying the beauty of what our daughter used to call "dark morning," that time just before sunrise. I was enjoying a cup of hot tea and listening to the birds wake up and greet each other in song. As I looked over the field toward the sunrise, the silhouette of a huge maple blocked my view. As it became lighter, the starkness or nakedness of the tree began to stand out.

The tree has tiny buds but no leaves. It will have them soon, and then it will be beautiful and bring shade to our deck and the chairs that we sit in under it. But not now. Now it is naked of all that beauty.

I thought our lives are like that before the Lord. When the Lord created us, we were naked. Then Adam chose to disobey God, and sin entered the world. One of the first things recorded was that God sewed fig leaves and clothed Adam and Eve. God covered their nakedness physically. God still covers our nakedness spiritually. Nothing in our lives is hidden before Him. It is like we stand behind a powerful X-ray machine that exposes every bone in our body; our hearts and thoughts are like this before Him. The Bible tells us that He even knows our thoughts before we think them.

Yet He loves us, He created us, and He has given us a covering through faith in His Son, Jesus. The Bible says that the blood of Jesus cleanses us from all sin. It washes us and makes our sin white as snow. Jesus takes away our shame and creates a vessel, a person of beauty from our broken, naked lives. Then our lives will be fruitful and bring blessings to others. The Lord is so wonderful; how can we not love and serve Him?

# 37

## MORE SPRING FLOWERS

ဆာ *Spring 2015* ၊ၑ

I have the most beautiful bouquet of spring flowers on our kitchen table. Pink and lavender hyacinth, yellow and white daffodils, multicolored tulips: they are so beautiful, and each one has its own fragrance. God created each one so unique, different, and beautiful to the eye. Alone, each one has its own beauty, but put them together and you have a bouquet!

I think people are like that. They are individuals, each one unique, but a family, friendship, or community can be like a bouquet. We each just have to see the individual and value and appreciate them, then understand that putting them together in a marriage, a family, or a community can be beautiful. But we first have to see the value and beauty that God has created in our own lives and let Him help us see that in others.

Just as different flowers have different fragrances, people have different personalities. If we appreciate those who are different—perhaps look different and speak differently—our lives can be enriched and not threatened.

God has created us to be loving and accepting. How do I know? Because those are two of the things that each of us desire in our own lives. And it seems that one of the principles of life that God has written in our hearts is that in order to receive it, you first must give it.

# 38

## MORNING TEA

**ളഠ** *June 15, 2016* **ദ**

Mitch and I drink hot tea every morning. This morning as I was making our tea and breakfast, I was in a hurry. Mitch was leaving early. I usually get up enough before him that I have a cup and sit outside.

Not today.

So I made the tea, and we sat down for our devotions, and I took my first drink. My tea was lukewarm. Uck.

Mitch and I enjoy our chai. After nine years in India, we brought the taste home with us. Now we even have Indian grocers that are near enough that we can shop there when our craving for Indian food becomes too great.

This morning when I made the tea, I did everything the same. We use an authentic Indian loose tea blend; I had heated the water and set the tea to steep. But it was terrible. Why?

I was in a hurry and did not wait for the water to reach that point where the heat would release the tea leaves' rich flavor. The water was hot enough for the color but not the flavor. It was flavor I was after.

Our lives can be like that.

James 1:2–3 says, "My brethren, count it all joy when ye fall into diverse temptations; Knowing this, that the trying of your faith worketh patience."

As a Christian, we will have temptations. The Bible says so. But these have a purpose. The purpose?

"Let perseverance finish its work so that you may be mature and complete, not lacking anything" (James 1:4).

God does have a purpose for our lives. His desire is that we reflect His character by our faith and obedience. How does He do that? One way is to refine us.

Similar to my tea, in order for us to be refined, many times the water (temptation) may—must be—a temperature high enough to release our flavor (surrender). Then God can work patience, which will leave us "mature and complete, not lacking anything."

# 39

## JUST SOME MORE
## THOUGHTS THIS MORNING

❧ *Summer 2016* ☙

Sometimes our roots have to go deep to grow.

This morning as I was watering some hens 'n' chickens that I have kept over the winter, I noticed a tall leafy stem that was not part of them. I gently pulled it from the soil so as not to disturb the other roots. When I pulled this stem out, the root was much longer than the actual plant. This little green, leafy plant had to grow up a very long way to reach the sunlight to grow.

I thought about how there can be times in our lives like that. They are usually painful times when our faith roots must be very deep so that we can grow toward the Son's light and work through our hurts. It is our roots that will sustain us when we haven't reached the top yet, when we still feel as though we are plowed under with hurt and pain. Difficult times will cause our roots to go deep if we seek the Lord during that time, and it is our deep roots that will sustain us during those times. It is a win-win for us.

Sometimes life isn't easy; it is painful at every turn. It is full of risks: to love our spouses, our children, and friends. When we open our hearts to others, it allows them access to the most tender, vulnerable part of who we are, and sometimes we get hurt. Sometimes it may even be us who are the ones doing the hurting of others.

But unless we are willing to open our hearts and be willing to expose our hearts to others, we will probably never know the deep, abiding love of Jesus. Because it is there in the deep part of our lives when we hurt and cry out to Him to sustain us, to help us grow through this, that we find Him and all that He brings: kindness, acceptance, healing for the hurt, and forgiveness for those who have hurt us. And we walk away wrapped in the assurance of His tender love for us.

Yes, life isn't easy, but it is precious. If we will let God's Spirit work in our lives, we will be richer for it, and maybe, just maybe, those around us will be too.

# 40

## DAYDREAMING

&#8286; *Summer 2009* &#8286;

Sometimes I daydream. One day recently I was praying for some people, and I was wishing there was a way to help. I had thought that if I had a million dollars (I realize I am not the only one with this daydream!), I could help so many people.

The thought actually caught on, and I began to mentally spend the million. Should I give one hundred people $100,000 each or one thousand people $1,000? I opted for door #2. I put a lot of thought into this over a few days. I would try not to let people I was helping know it was me. It was so much fun, then I ran out of money.

Hmm.

My daydream lost its glitter and enjoyment. Then I felt the Lord begin to speak to my heart.

Wanting to help others is a good thing. It originates from the Lord at work in my heart. But to just daydream and wait for or want something to just fall out of the sky was not profitable. I began to realize God had already begun to move my heart to help the ones that I wanted to help with the million dollars. Maybe I didn't have the money, but I did have that dozen eggs I felt the Lord speak to my heart to take to a neighbor, and I could babysit when I didn't feel like it (which is worth more than money to the tired mommy).

The more I thought on it, the more I saw that yes, money would be nice (okay, great!), but I didn't need millions to touch people's lives. I just needed to be sensitive to God at work in my heart to meet the kind of need in a person's life that money just can't buy. It is called *caring*.

And yes, I can do that.

Thank you, Lord, for your wonderful work in our hearts that help us live our lives to the fullest—right here, right now. No daydream needed.

# 41

## SOME THOUGHTS ON GETTING A 'LITTLE LOST'

ᔕ *August 28, 2009* ᦉ

I got lost today. I wasn't totally lost; I knew I would find my way home. My husband says that no one can get really lost in Illinois since all roads lead north/south or east/west. But country roads can be deceiving.

I was on my way home from town sixteen miles away. It was a beautiful evening, so I decided to take the country road, not the one I usually take, and enjoy the scenery: cornfields, pastures with cows, and wildflowers. Then I got distracted and took a wrong turn. I looked up and everything looked familiar, but I didn't know where I was. I recognized road signs, but I had no idea where they would lead. I was on a country road that was surrounded by ten-foot-high cornfields. I felt very alone. I didn't like the feeling.

I did know that if I just headed in the right direction, I would eventually know where I was. I could get home. So I drove and drove and drove.

I thought that this is what happens to us sometimes as Christians. We are headed somewhere good spiritually, and then we get distracted. We look up and realize that we are in unfamiliar territory and feel lost. We question, "Where are you, Lord? Why can't I see my way?" We are surrounded by ten-foot-high cornfields. Things may seem familiar, and we are in fellowship with the Lord, but we aren't sure where it is going.

When I realized that I was lost and didn't want to go on not knowing where I was going, I prayed out loud. "Heavenly Father, I am lost. Please show me the right road to take to get home." The very next turn led me to the road home. I thought, "Wow, I should have prayed sooner!"

It is like that in our spiritual lives also. When we get distracted and feel lost, if we will turn our hearts to Him in prayer and cry out, He will answer. He promised.

# 42

FIELDS

❧ *September 18, 2012* ☙

On my way into town today, I passed by miles and miles of corn and soybean fields. They are a thing of beauty to me. I guess it is just the Midwest that is in my blood. Some of the fields are being harvested. It is my favorite time of the year.

This morning as I was passing by, I realized something that I had never thought about before. The fields are mature. The harvest is only for the mature fields. I felt the Lord spoke to my heart about our lives as believers. The Word of God tells us that unless a grain of wheat falls into the ground and dies, it abides alone (John 12:24). Something has to die in order for life to come from it.

Have you ever looked at a mature cornfield? The corn is dead. The field is brown, and the stalks are shriveled. It looks lifeless, but it is only then that it can be harvested, after it has matured.

Isn't that such an analogy of our life in Christ? But I have never thought about the harvest in that way. The harvest is the reaping of the sowing. It is the harvest that is important. It doesn't matter how much corn is planted: if there is no harvest, there is no profit.

It is like that with us. It is the harvest that God is looking for in our lives. The Word calls it *fruit*. The Lord is interested in the fruit of our lives. But if it takes dying to produce a harvest, how do we do that? How do we die to produce? It will be different with each one of us, but it will have to happen in order for the harvest of our lives.

Two days ago, September 16, marked the anniversary of the birth and death of our second daughter, Katie (Kathryn Ruth). She died at birth. She was premature, just like our first daughter, Amy; Elisabeth, our third daughter; and me. I wanted to write and tell her story, but I couldn't. I didn't want to share that with anyone. She would be twenty-six years old. If all of our children would have lived, they would be stairsteps: twenty-four, twenty-five, twenty-six, twenty-seven, and twenty-eight years old. Only one lived, Elisabeth. She is twenty-four and the mother of two precious little girls.

I was sharing this because I realized this morning that much of the harvest of my life has come from death and broken places. The Lord has allowed these things. I know I am not alone. Many, many have suffered great loss, but in my life, these are things that God has used to help me die. Not physically, but to my own selfish interests, self-centeredness, and pride. I am grateful for this. I think it has made me a better person. Death is the one thing that we cannot undo. It is final. One out of every one person dies.

When we are faced with circumstances that are beyond our control, we often turn to the Lord; we seek help and grace for what we need to cope. I did that each time. Did it get easier? I don't think so. I think I just grew in my faith and trust in His loving care for me, and I was able to grow, and God was at work producing a harvest in my life.

Yes, I can understand how we must die before we can mature so that our lives can produce a harvest—and I am grateful.

# 43

## GRANDDAUGHTERS

*ঙ July 2008 ৫*

What a blessing! Our seven-month-old granddaughter spent the night with us last night (and slept through the night! Always a plus!). I have just fed her and put her down on the floor. She is learning to crawl. It usually begins from a sitting position and moves to an on-her-face position. This is achieved by a gentle rolling on the floor or a thud as she lands! Then she instinctively draws her knees up and starts pushing. She will take a break from her labor and look up, just to make sure I am still there watching.

Sometimes, I will put toys just out of her reach so she will reach. She pats the floor and talks. No, I cannot understand the words, but you can see they have meaning for her. She is intentional. This is a very big deal. This is becoming mobile. It takes effort and practice. For months, her mommy has been putting her on a blanket for tummy time. The goal was to strengthen her little arms, preparing her to crawl. God has given her the instinct, but she has to learn to use her arms and legs and strengthen her muscles. When she takes her first crawling steps, we will all clap and encourage her. Right now, she can only move in reverse! She has not learned the forward gear, but she will.

I see so many parallels to the Christian life. When we are learning in our walk with the Lord, there are usually two ways we come to the place of falling on our faces before Him. We can gently roll, or sometimes we fall with a thud. But that is the place we have to come to before we can go on.

Instinctively, we pull up on our knees (or fall on our knees) to move forward and usually end up going in reverse before we move forward. The Lord will teach us by putting what we want just out of our reach, so that we will reach. Prayer is the key. It takes practice and work. We will learn how to pray by using our prayer muscles. That is, our fellowship with our Heavenly Father will deepen through prayer. And just like a child, when we raise our eyes just to see if He is watching, we will be encouraged by the Lord in a way that speaks to our hearts, to show us that He is there watching, clapping, and encouraging.

# 44

## A GOOD NEWS STORY

*ઓ March 12, 2009 ૯ૹ*

I volunteer weekly at our local Christian radio station, WLLM. This is Thursday, my volunteer day. Today I met Bethel. The station is having their fundraiser, so the listeners are invited to come into the station for lunch to get to know each other and the staff.

Bethel is an escapee, as such. I was a greeter today, so I met her at the door. She told me she was ninety-six years old. She is recovering from a stroke a few months back and still has some visual facial abnormalities. (She has a very sweet crooked smile, but she still smiled all morning!) She told me she had left her metal walker in a corridor at the nursing home (so the metal detector wouldn't go off as she left) and had a friend pick her up and bring her to the station. (Yes, I was a bit concerned that I might be aiding and abetting, but what to do?)

As we were talking, I was a little afraid to just leave her in case she lost her balance, so I sat beside her and talked to her. I noticed her wedding ring and commented on it. I already knew she was a widow; she told me she continued to wear it to keep the wolves away. She said that men at the nursing home were always asking her to marry them; she is not interested.

She had had a very hard life. Because she was ill when she was only two, she had to be put into a children's home. She wasn't able to leave until she was thirty years old. (This was almost seventy years ago.) She then met her husband, who made her life "like a fairy tale." They raised four boys together. He died in 2002, and she is now in a nursing home. I was thinking that if I had chosen not to reach out to her, I would have missed this sweet woman's story.

I hope that her story has brought a smile to your face as it did mine, so I am sharing it with you. And I would encourage you to be sensitive to those the Lord brings across your path. We never know the hidden treasure in the lives of those around us. It just takes a little of our time and caring to see it.

Have a wonderful day!

# 45

## IN CLOSING

In Closing,

I want to thank you for taking the time to read my journal. These life lessons have come over several decades in my life. And they have not stopped! I am still learning as I now enter into my seventieth year.

I am so grateful that God does not just put us on a shelf to dry out. He uses everything in our lives to teach us how to live fuller lives and to use these Life Lessons to bless others and help them on their way.

If this book has been a blessing, I am grateful.

Thank you again, and may God bless you as you seek Him.

Gratefully His,

*Linda Kropp*
Spring 2024